A FAMILY
OUTING

A FAMILY OUTING

A MEMOIR

RUBY REMENDA SWANSON

Cormorant Books

Canada Council **Conseil des Arts**
for the Arts **du Canada**

 ONTARIO ARTS COUNCIL
CONSEIL DES ARTS DE L'ONTARIO
an Ontario government agency
un organisme du gouvernement de l'Ontario

 Canadian Patrimoine
Heritage canadien   Canadä

The publisher gratefully acknowledges the support of the Canada Council for the Arts and the
Ontario Arts Council for its publishing program. We acknowledge the financial support of the
Government of Canada through the Canada Book Fund (CBF) for our publishing activities, and
the Government of Ontario through the Ontario Media Development Corporation, an agency
of the Ontario Ministry of Culture, and the Ontario Book Publishing Tax Credit Program.

LIBRARY AND ARCHIVES CANADA CATALOGUING IN PUBLICATION

Swanson, Ruby Remenda, 1954–, author
A family outing : a memoir / Ruby Remenda Swanson.

Issued in print and electronic formats.
ISBN 978-1-77086-476-4 (paperback). — ISBN 978-1-77086-481-8 (html)

1. Swanson, Ruby Remenda, 1954–. 2. Swanson, Ruby Remenda, 1954– — Family.
3. Parents of gays -- Canada. 4. Coming out (Sexual orientation) — Canada.
5. Gay teenagers — Family relationships — Canada: 6. Mothers and sons.
1. Title.

HQ759.9145.S93 2016   306.874'3   C2016-904414-9
                                           C2016-904415-7

Cover design: angeljohnguerra.com
Interior text design: Tannice Goddard, bookstopress.com
Printer: Friesens

Printed and bound in Canada.

 MIX
Paper from
responsible sources
FSC   FSC® C016245
www.fsc.org

The interior of this book is printed on 100% post-consumer waste recycled paper.

CORMORANT BOOKS INC.
10 ST. MARY STREET, SUITE 615, TORONTO, ONTARIO, M4Y 1P9
www.cormorantbooks.com

In memory of Uncle Fred and Uncle Jerry,
who had to hide

Contents

In 2002 when my sixteen-year-old son, Carl, came to my office and told me he was gay, my initial reaction was shock, fear, and denial. I looked for a book that would help me cope with the news, provide me with encouragement, and prepare me for what might be coming. I did not find anything that spoke to how I felt or to the type of experiences our family was beginning to have.

It would have been inconceivable in those early weeks and months for me to think that a decade later I'd be writing the very book I had been looking for, one that would help others who find themselves in the same situation as I did. It was at the insistence of one of my colleagues with whom I periodically carpool that I began to write down my feelings and thoughts. On the Family Day weekend in February 2011 I made a list of forty-six experiences I thought I could write about. Then I started typing. Some stories and descriptions were six pages long and others were only three sentences, but the list of things to write about kept getting longer.

I wrote about what it was like to hear my child tell me he was gay and how I reacted the first time I saw him kissing his boyfriend. I addressed the deeply homophobic time in which I grew up. I started digging into our family histories and learned about my gay great uncles. I learned more about the AIDS epidemic and how it transformed the lesbian, gay, bisexual, and transgender (LGBT) landscape in North America. I wrote about attending a drag queen show. I described the nearly uncontrollable rage I felt toward protestors at anti same-sex marriage rallies.

Writing about the experiences I had as the Edmonton Director of Parents, Families and Friends of Lesbians and Gays (PFLAG) reminded me of how good it felt to be able to help someone by simply making a few phone calls — such as the time I found a gay men's social group for a fifty-six-year-old man who had just come out. I wrote about going to an annual general meeting to discuss the future of the gay and lesbian centre in Edmonton and coming home a few hours later as the only straight person on the interim executive board of what would become the Pride Centre of Edmonton.

Through many years of participating in panel presentations about coming out, I listened to personal testimonials by many LGBT individuals and their families. I wrote about what happens to our children as they come out to themselves and how this step influences their coming out to others. No child wants to lose his or her family, friends — the people in their lives they love. This makes the initial coming out to family one of the most sensitive, emotionally charged, stressful, and unpredictable situations our gay children have to navigate in their lives.

A Family Outing addresses the range of pain and heartache families endure, such as when we realize our sons and daughters could be the victims of discrimination or hate crimes for simply being who they are. It also provides positive perspectives, including recent gains in recognition and acceptance of same-sex marriage and the establishment of gay/straight alliances in schools.

A year and a half after my son came out, Carl was on the other side of the country at the University of Toronto, where he's lived ever since. It wasn't because he was at my side that I took on LGBT advocacy. My entry point for activism was the Canadian same-sex marriage legislation debate. The pro-same-sex marriage side had to be represented and supported by the straight community so I became involved by publicly advocating for equality and acceptance of my son and fellow human beings like him. In the years that followed I met and worked on all sorts of LGBT issues with extraordinarily brave LGBT activists and true heroes. The LGBT community is made up of our own sons and daughters, best friends, coworkers, neighbours, favourite aunts and uncles, and our brothers and sisters, all of whom now and in this country are no longer sentenced from birth to hide who they are, although they may not find acceptance in every part of their lives. My book is about being an advocate, helping others, standing up to taunts from religious fundamentalists and political protestors, and holding people accountable for their treatment of the LGBT community. It's a story about the discrimination gay people still face today.

My family has been fortunate. My gay son has not endured years of bullying and psychological damage. There were no suicide attempts or episodes of despair. My family's experiences have been mostly positive, although there has been some heartache. This book is about overcoming the fears I had, fears which were based on attitudes from the deeply homophobic time of my high school years in the 1960s and seventies and in the frightening years of the AIDS epidemic in the 1980s and nineties. It's about what I learned from other parents, members of the LGBT community, advocates, historians, and my own family. It's about my personal growth to becoming a public advocate for the wider LGBT community.

As I was writing, my son, Paul, who's straight, regularly reminded me, "Everyone who's coming out needs a book to give to their parents. They need your book." I don't have all the answers, but it is my hope by writing about my experiences and what I've learned along the way, I'll be providing help to those people who are in their own process of navigating gay.

Part One

I

Coming Out

CIDER HOUSE 〜

OUR SON CARL WAS IN HIS MID-TEENS THE DECEMBER AFTERNOON I TRIED to have a conversation with him about the movie *The Cider House Rules*. The night before, his dad and I had watched it on TV. Carl had unlimited interest in good movies, loved talking about them, and would watch everything from *Toy Story* to *Gone with the Wind* to *Scream*. I was certain he'd want to hear about the movie. Seeing that I had a teenaged son who may or may not have been sexually active at the time, my other motive was to use the movie to talk about situations surrounding unplanned pregnancies.

Our two sons didn't have a sister, which left me with the task of introducing them to at least some of the basic facts of life from a female perspective. Throughout their lives I had deliberately talked about contraception, menstrual cramps, menopause, and what it felt like for me to be pregnant and give birth. I wanted them to have an idea of what girls and women experienced every month of their lives for forty years and what it was like for women when our bodies wound down the capacity to reproduce.

With that in mind I launched into what I thought was a Saturday afternoon candid talk about pregnancy, childbirth, and adoption as depicted in *Cider House*. Conversations with both sons were usually short and to the point. That afternoon Carl was lying on the couch reading in the living room. I was cleaning up the kitchen, well within speaking range. "Dad

3

and I watched *The Cider House Rules* last night," I said. "It won a couple of Academy Awards. I think you'd like it."

"Oh yeah? What's it about?"

"An orphanage in the 1940s. It's run by a nice old doctor played by Michael Caine. Tobey Maguire is abandoned as a baby and grows up there."

"He was in *Pleasantville*."

"The other characters are mostly girls and women who get pregnant. Some of them go to the orphanage to have the babies and leave them there to be adopted and others go there to have abortions."

"Sounds like a serious movie."

He wasn't showing the kind of interest I had hoped for. I continued from the kitchen.

"The main female character is a young woman who goes to the orphanage to have an abortion before her boyfriend goes off to war. He comes back from the war paralyzed from the waist down. It's really heartbreaking."

"You don't have to worry," Carl snapped. "I'll never get a girl pregnant!" Throwing his arms out in front of him, he jumped up off the couch and fled to his room.

I stayed in the kitchen trying to figure out what made him go from indifference to hostility in one breath. He wasn't the kind of kid who overreacted or stormed out of a room in a snit because I interrupted him while he was reading or playing a video game. At the very least I had expected to have a conversation with him about why the movie had won awards. I was hoping it would lead to a discussion about sexual activity and had prepared myself to hear reassurances such as, "Don't worry, I'll be careful," or at worst "I'm not that stupid." He eventually came back downstairs and I let it go.

That evening while my husband, Leonard, and I were sitting in bed reading, I told him about Carl's outburst. "I don't know what set him off. Do you think he might be gay?"

"I think you're reading too much into this," Leonard said, barely paying attention to me. Sometimes conversations with Leonard were also short and to the point. There was no more discussion and the thought passed from my mind.

NIGHT TERRORS ∽

WHEN I WAS GROWING up, everyone at our house had some sort of minor sleep disorder. Three people talked in their sleep, one was a sleepwalker, one ground her teeth, and two snored so loudly the windows rattled. I was accustomed to lots of noise and people walking around in the middle of the night.

As a little boy, Carl would sometimes walk and talk in his sleep. When he was seven years old, he sleepwalked all the way down the stairs. I woke up when I heard him walking back upstairs. In the morning we found the kitchen door wide open. We had no way of knowing whether or not he had gone outside that night. I worried a bit when it happened but it didn't alarm me because it is what I had grown up with. This was normal.

In grade ten, Carl had five or six severe night terrors over a two-month period. This wasn't the same as a preschooler who was having a bad dream that I could hold in my arms to settle. Even with my childhood familiarity with sleepwalkers and talkers, I had no experience with night terrors. One night as Carl was violently thrashing around and screaming in his bed, he kicked a hole in the wall. Another night he rolled down an entire flight of stairs without waking up. It also happened once at my mother's house. At two thirty in the morning, Carl was standing in the middle of her living room screaming. Leonard and I bolted out of bed and turned on all the lights. I planted myself in front of my son, grabbed his shoulders, shook him, and shouted, "Carl, wake up! It's okay, Carl, wake up!" Panting as if he had run a marathon, he stopped screaming and held his forehead in his hand. He let me take him back to the bedroom and he got back into bed. I covered him up. He settled immediately and slept through to the morning. It was the same each time: eyes wide open, arms and legs flailing, desperate, nonsensical screaming.

My mom stayed in her bed and calmly said, "Go back to sleep." I'm sure she spent the rest of the night praying the rosary.

In the morning I told her about the night terrors. "We don't know what's going on. This isn't the first time this has happened. We don't know what to do." Mom had no advice.

The morning after the terrors, Carl would wake up and tell us he had dreamt we were being attacked and he was trying to save us from bombs.

Years later he said, "I still remember everything about the nightmares. They were terrifying."

His dad and I had no idea why the night terrors were happening. We wondered if there were problems with his friends, or if he was stressed about his first year of high school. Down the street the father of one of his classmates was dying as a result of a brain tumour. Since Leonard had had cancer twice, we speculated this fear could be causing the sleep demons. We talked to his teachers at the winter parent-teacher conferences. "Is Carl getting along with everyone? Is anything going on in class that could be triggering this?" The teachers said everything was going well at school. His phys. ed. teacher told us his four-year-old daughter had night terrors, but had no advice.

We didn't know what to do. Although two months was not a long time, after the second and third incident I looked for professional advice. I made appointments for both Leonard and me to see a counselor through the Employee Assistance program at work, and for Carl to go on his own. The visits were not particularly helpful. "Give it time," the counselor recommended. We left baffled. The night terrors ended as mysteriously as they started. Carl came out to his dad a few months later.

DECEMBER 4, 2002 ↜

I WAS AT WORK, sitting at my desk in the physics department at the University of Alberta working on lab renovation floor plans, when the phone rang.

"Hi Mom. It's Carl. I want to come see you after school."

"Sure, I'll be in my office. See you soon, bye." The exchange lasted less than ten seconds.

Within minutes I began to worry. He'd never called me like this before. What does he want to talk about that can't wait until I get home from work, I wondered. Why does he need to come to my office? Don't overreact, I told myself. But I knew this was something serious. I created scenarios that became worse and worse by the hour. It was one thirty-five in the afternoon. He had called in between classes from his school, where he was in grade eleven.

I closed the door and called Leonard to see if he knew what was going on, but he wasn't at his desk. The next couple of hours crawled. I tried to work, but couldn't focus. Had Carl banged up the car? Was there a problem at school? He had never had problems at school and had a great group of friends. He didn't have a girlfriend, so it was unlikely he was going to tell me he got someone pregnant.

Close to four o'clock Carl came into my office and closed the door. He didn't unzip his ski jacket or sit down. He leaned against the door with his toque and gloves in one hand and the doorknob in the other, leading me to think he didn't intend to stay too long.

"How was school today?" I asked.

"I'm worried about Eric. He's being stupid." Eric was one of his closest friends. Although I felt like saying, "Just tell me what's going on Carl, I've been going crazy trying to figure out what's up since you called," this time I knew I had to be patient. The first thing to pop into my head about Eric was I hoped it was just another speeding ticket and not a fender bender. Eric drove to school on Whitemud Drive, a small stretch of freeway in Edmonton. Earlier in the fall he had received a couple of black and white photos of the back of his mom's car compliments of the Edmonton City Police photo radar unit. I listened, thinking, whatever he's here about has nothing to do with Eric.

Still leaning against the door and obviously stalling, Carl told me he was relieved Andre, the exchange student who had lived with us for three months that fall, had gone back home. "It's nice to have our house back to just our family," he mumbled. This wasn't about Andre, either. My boy looked tired. Clearly he had something serious he needed to tell me. Not moving to sit down but acting like he was ready to leave he looked directly at me. Slowly and sadly, without blinking or looking away, he said, "I'm gay."

"Well, that's okay," I replied instantly, and I meant it. When things at our house were not okay or bad, it meant another cancer reoccurrence. Being gay was okay, but what he said stunned me. I didn't believe what I was hearing. I hadn't prepared for this scenario, not that afternoon, or at any time during his life. With the exception of the one brief moment a year or two earlier during the *Cider House Rules* talk, it had never occurred to me that I could have a gay child. My only thought was, "Why does he think he's gay?"

Carl leaned against the closed door and didn't move. "The part that sucks about this is I'll never be able to have kids," he said with deep sadness in his voice.

"Don't say that, Carl," I said without taking a breath and with as much conviction as I could find. "You don't know what life is going to be like fifteen years from now when it's time for you to have children." I didn't believe a word I was saying about the possibility of him being able to have a family. My child was despondent, and I had to say something to make him feel better.

I stood up, walked around my desk and held my boy in my arms. I didn't let go first. There were no tears, there was just silence. For the next hour we sat beside each other, together on the floor, in the corner of my office next to the coat rack, and talked while it got dark outside and the rest of the staff went home for the day. The floor was the right place because we could actually be close to each other, not because I didn't have enough chairs in my office. My handsome, six-foot-tall, 160-pound, sixteen-year-old son with beautiful blue eyes and a head full of loose, curly brown hair told me he had been avoiding this conversation for months.

"I told Dad first, at the beginning of the summer, and asked him not to tell you. I wanted to tell you when the time was right for me." With my arm around his broad shoulders and his head on my shoulder he added, "I'll tell Paul when the time is right. I don't want you to tell him before I do." I have no recollection of what else we talked about.

I called home to tell Leonard that Carl and I were going to Subway for a sandwich. I needed to be alone with him to process the news. We drove there in his car, Scooby, the kids' car, a white, two-door 1988 Ford Escort with Scooby Doo rubber floor mats. We plowed through the snow-piled Edmonton streets in the dark winter cold. I did my best to pretend I was fine and this was all normal. In reality I was dazed and in shock. The date was Wednesday, December 4, 2002.

Two weeks later I learned a same-sex couple in the neighbourhood next to ours had privately adopted a child. I thought — I'm clairvoyant! I started noticing same-sex news stories, paying attention to the details because these issues had become part of my life. This particular story made me happy because I wanted grandchildren.

Years later Carl told me he had deliberately waited until Andre had gone back home to Quebec before he told me. "I thought it would take you a bit of time to process this information. I didn't want to complicate things further for you by having a stranger in our house when I came out. That day at school, four days after Andre left, the pressure got to be too much to bear and I quickly decided to tell you."

Carl was right. It took the entire month of December for my shock to dissipate. At the same time, I wanted Carl to feel supported and to know his relationship with his dad and me was the same as it had always been. Carl and I went to a concert a couple of days later and over the Christmas holidays we tackled a several-thousand piece Lego project that took over the basement. I felt I needed time alone with him to demonstrate everything was okay with me. This likely did more good for me than it did for him; our kids were good at adapting to new things. Until then I had dealt with big changes and the trauma of Leonard's two bouts of cancer by talking to and getting support from family, friends, and medical professionals. This time Leonard and I relied mostly on each other until Carl eventually — seven months later — came out to his fourteen-year-old brother Paul.

I had never seriously suspected my son was gay. Many parents say things like, "I knew she was different from her sisters when she was eighteen months old," or "When he was five, I don't know why, but I just knew." This was not the case with Carl. For one thing, he is very much like his father. He doesn't look like his dad, but he thinks like his dad, acts like his dad, and sounds like his dad. Therefore, if my husband was not gay, how could Carl be gay?

For about a year and a half after Carl told me he was gay, I would often say to Leonard, "So, is there anything you want to talk about?" or "I know we've been busy for the last twenty-two years but is there anything on your mind?" I couldn't see how two people who were so similar could be so fundamentally different.

"I'm not gay," my husband assured me.

"Yeah, but how do you know?"

"Because I'm not gay."

"Do you ever wonder if you are gay?"

"No. I've always been attracted to women. I don't think it's likely that that's going to change."

SECRETS ⌣

WHEN CARL CAME OUT our two sons were at home with us in the same house Leonard and I have lived in since 1989. It's a sixty-five-year-old semi-bungalow on a street lined with beautiful, mature elm trees right beside the University of Alberta in Edmonton. I love to garden and have many flowerbeds, a few shrubs, and a tiny vegetable garden. Most of our neighbours are academics or medical professionals who work at the university hospital.

Carl and Paul, our sons, were always close — even though they are three years apart in age. During high school Carl always invited Paul along when he arranged elaborate themed activities such as his version of *The Amazing Race Edmonton*. The boys lived together again for a few years in Toronto while Paul attended Ryerson University and Carl attended the University of Toronto. When he came out, Carl was in grade eleven and Paul was in grade eight. It took a full year for him to come out to the three of us.

Years later, Carl explained how he made the decision to come out to me. "Most people are strategic. I deliberately didn't come out until I was sure I was gay. I could have come out in grade nine or ten and maybe would have said I was bi, but I wanted to be sure, so I waited. When I came out I wasn't guessing anymore.

"That day in school the pressure got to be too much — I had to stop keeping a secret and get it off my chest. Your reaction didn't matter anymore. My inaction made me feel worse than the action of having to tell you. But it didn't help when for weeks after you kept asking me if I was sure. I had resolved this with myself. I was sure."

Carl was three months away from his seventeenth birthday when he came out to me. He had always been levelheaded and mature and yet, in spite of that, I asked him on too many occasions if he was sure he was gay. Asking him if he was sure was not helpful. When he got to the point where he was having the conversation with me it should have been safe for me to assume he was sure.

I struggled to understand how my husband could have known something so important and kept it secret from me for five months. I felt betrayed. We knew pretty much everything there was to know about each other's dreams, fears, hopes, and worries. Our relationship had survived multiple bouts of cancer and a complete career change early in our marriage, which meant living on a single income while Leonard was in graduate school when we decided to have a baby. When Carl was four months old I couldn't bear the thought of leaving him with a babysitter. I got an extension on my maternity leave that allowed me to be at home with him for ten months. Having my mat leave extended didn't help. Two weeks after the extension was approved I quit a job I loved with the Canadian Broadcasting Corporation (CBC) to stay at home with my baby. We had mortgage payments, an infant, and no jobs. Neither of our families could afford to help us financially if Leonard wasn't able to find a job and we found ourselves penniless.

Leonard, the boys, and I always liked being together. The four of us were particularly good at long car trips. Before Leonard and I had kids we drove back and forth across Canada and the US among Saskatchewan, Detroit, and New York several times. We did this because of summer jobs and to visit our families. Leonard and I met in 1979 at the Saskatchewan Summer School of the Arts located in the Qu'Appelle Valley, a forty-five-minute drive from Regina. I arrived a day early to get settled in for the summer. I checked in with the office to see which dorm I was assigned to, unloaded a couple pieces of luggage, parked my car and went down to the dining hall for lunch. The hall could seat two hundred, but there was only one table with people at it; the rest of the summer staff and instructors had not yet arrived. Luckily, there was room at the table for one more so I joined the handful of early arrivals.

I had a long history with the summer school; it started in 1970 when I was a high school drama student. The first time I sat down in the dining hall with my tray I realized I didn't know how to use a knife and fork properly. My mother always overcooked everything so there was no need for us to learn how to use a table knife. We could cut through everything using the side of our fork. In the mid-seventies I had summer jobs there as a dorm supervisor and secretary in the office. The kitchen staff used to heap our plates with food. In 1979 we served ourselves and chose what we wanted to eat and the size of the serving. As always, people complained about the awful institutional food.

The day I arrived at the summer school in '79 was perfect weather for the beach. At lunchtime in the dining room I recognized one person, the director. He introduced me to the others at the table who were all men and all musicians. I met the head of the Music program, the chain-smoking office manager, two set-up and teardown crewmembers, and Leonard, the tuba player from New York, who was one of the band instructors. Leonard invited me to drive into the nearby town of Fort Qu'Appelle with him after lunch. He needed to buy a bathing suit so we could go swimming in Echo Lake. That's how our life together started: lunch and an afternoon at the beach. Three weeks later Leonard's teaching contract was over. We promised each other we would keep in touch. As he was driving away from the summer school he looked in the back seat of his mom's car and realized he had left one of his instruments behind. Unknown to me he turned the car around and snuck back into the studio to pick up his other horn.

Meanwhile, I stood in the veranda of my dorm staring out over the vast lawn. I stood there for a long time listening to the sound of orchestra students practising excerpts and doing scales on their instruments and thought — what just happened here? I miss him already. Leonard drove to his parents' home where he dropped off his mom's car before going back to New York. Two months later he came back to see me and we got engaged. We had a major problem. Leonard was living in New York City and I was in Saskatoon. We were engaged, had spent less than a month together in the same location, and we were getting to know each other over the phone and through letters. After a few months I solved the problem. I sold everything I owned, except for the eight boxes of clothes and cookbooks that fit into my red 1976 Volkswagen Rabbit, and drove to New York. We were married in Detroit in April 1980. We went back to work at the Summer School as a married couple the following summer. Six years later we had Carl and three years after that Paul was born.

Leonard grew up in Grosse Pointe, Michigan, which at that time was an overwhelmingly white suburb of Detroit. He was a University of Michigan music grad, had attended Julliard, and was freelancing in New York when we met. We lived in Manhattan and New Jersey for two years before moving to Canada, where Leonard played tuba with the Calgary Philharmonic Orchestra and I worked in the Public Affairs Office at the University of Calgary. I loved visiting New York, but never got used to living there and was very happy when a job came up for

Leonard in Calgary. We moved to Edmonton in 1983 for Leonard to attend graduate school at U of A and have lived there ever since.

Over the years, Leonard, the boys, and I spent hundreds of hours in the car driving back and forth from Edmonton to Saskatchewan to visit my family. We drove to Detroit for Leonard's twenty-year high school reunion in 1995. A few years later we drove to Atlanta, Georgia, via New York City and Washington, DC for a family reunion in 2000. The four of us, and Rhett our Jack Russell Terrier, travelled nearly ten thousand kilometres in three and a half weeks in our '91 Volkswagen Westfalia van. The poor dog was miserable. Later, Leonard and I drove to Toronto with Carl's stuff for his first year at the University of Toronto. We took the long route through Ontario to see the Terry Fox Memorial in Thunder Bay. On the way home we picked up Paul in northern Michigan where he had spent the summer at the Interlochen Music Camp.

Despite all our practice at coming through major difficulties and temporary challenges together, when Leonard kept Carl's secret, I felt that since he's my husband, the father of our children, my best friend, and soulmate, he should have told me. He had supported me through paralyzing homesickness and immigration obstacles when we lived in New York and was my strongest cheerleader years later when I switched jobs and careers. I felt he hadn't let me be a support for him in a family situation when we most needed each other.

Keeping Carl's secret was debilitating for Leonard. It was particularly painful for him when he read LGBT newspaper and magazine articles. For months he couldn't share his fears and anguish with me and alone had faced the same emotions and uncertainties I was feeling. Leonard explained, "This was way beyond the most serious thing I had ever had to deal with in my life. I wasn't going to screw it up by betraying Carl's confidence because I needed to talk to you about a newspaper story and could have accidently let something slip. Carl had to do this on his schedule, when he felt comfortable. He needed to figure out when the time was right for him."

A few months after Carl came out to me I ran into an old roommate. I hadn't seen her since we shared the main floor of a house in the late seventies. We made a lunch date. During the hour and a half we took for lunch we talked about our jobs, travels, family illnesses and deaths, and caught up on two decades of life. She had always been wise. I needed advice on how to handle the way I felt about Leonard keeping a secret from me. Carl, Leonard, and I were still "in the closet." As far as I knew, no one had told Paul.

I explained that I couldn't be specific, but one of our sons had shared something very personal with Leonard. Leonard hadn't told me because our son instructed him not to. I couldn't believe Leonard had kept a secret about one of our children from me. I was hurt. I felt betrayed.

My friend's advice was abrupt and straightforward. It was clear she was taking Leonard's side. Leonard was secure in our relationship. He had no choice but to honour our son's wishes. She then said, "It sounds like by doing anything else he could have jeopardized his relationship with one of the boys." I sat there without saying a word. She then matter-of-factly ordered, "Let it go. This isn't a problem." With my teeth clenched, I flopped back in my chair and stared at the restaurant's sky-blue ceiling. She was right; what was going on was about Carl, not about me. Leonard and I had to do what was right for our son. Nevertheless, the months of secrecy and deception, during the time Carl was not out to his brother, had a demoralizing effect on my soul.

Each winter, after enduring up to three months of freezing cold temperatures with fifteen hours of darkness every day, I crave to be outside in my yard. I spend hundreds of hours every year working in my tiny vegetable garden and ever-expanding flowerbeds. I love days in early spring when it's so warm I can be outside in a T-shirt while shoveling snow. People who live in warmer climates think western Canadians are crazy, but five degrees Celsius feels warm after the deep freeze of winter. On one of those beautiful spring days, I was in the backyard moving around piles of snow so it would melt more quickly. While I spread shovelfuls of snow on my flowerbeds, I eagerly cleared away last year's fallen leaves from other beds to see if I could spot any sprouting bulbs. I quietly wept while I searched for signs of spring.

Leonard, returning home from work, came through the back gate. "Why are you crying?" he asked calmly.

I told him that it felt as if my soul was being destroyed. I had this secret, and I didn't know why it was a secret. Why did having a gay child have to be a carefully disclosed piece of information? I couldn't stop myself. Why was it so hard for Carl to tell Paul? Why were we afraid for Carl and Paul's safety? Why would anyone be threatened by someone who is gay? Why were we parking our car around the corner from the gay and lesbian centre when we attended a support group meeting? Why was I lying to Paul about going to a support group? Why was I worried about how my mom would react?

I've never had to hide anything about myself because I was afraid of what would happen if others knew. Now, because Carl was not out to his brother, I couldn't talk to anyone but his dad about this part of our lives. I couldn't risk at some time in the future Paul saying to me, "You talked about it to Baba, or Judy and Margaret before anyone told me." I felt isolated and alone. I cried for weeks, which turned into months, as I began to navigate having a gay son.

The day I found out Carl was gay, I also learned he had come out to his friend Lisa. A couple of weeks earlier, the two had gone for coffee and while walking along trendy Whyte Avenue they agreed one of the boys at school, who was a mutual friend, was cute. Lisa casually asked Carl how long he had known he was bi.

Carl corrected her, telling her that he wasn't bi. He was gay. They kept walking and talking. Lisa accepted this information and until the following summer was the only person Carl's age who he had come out to. Coming out to Lisa went smoothly whether it was unplanned or maybe only partially planned.

Not long after Carl came out to me, he left for a language exchange in Quebec for three months. While he was in Quebec, Carl counseled me to talk to someone. He suggested that I should talk to Lisa. Lisa was a friend Carl had made in high school. I had met Lisa a few times before when the kids were doing homework projects together at our house.

Carl and Lisa had already spoken about this possibility and she had agreed to meet me for coffee, although she wasn't sure what she could say to me to help me understand and stop worrying.

We met on campus in the Students' Union Building at U of A. Lisa was a smart, levelheaded girl who had several pieces of advice for me. She told me that for her, Carl was a friend she'd made relatively recently, in high school, and so everything about him was new to her. Finding out he was gay was like finding out everything else about him, like the fact he played piano. Whether or not someone was gay wasn't an issue for Lisa. Then she said something unexpected for a person so young; she said that it would take me a little while to get used to this new fact about Carl because I'd known him so well already. What an insightful kid, I thought.

Carl's sexuality was simply something different than what I had assumed for his entire life — until now. My son was the same person he'd always been. In time, I would get used to it. What could I say? I studied her and wondered how a sixteen year old could be so wise.

I had more issues I needed to thrash out. Carl and I were arguing because he wanted to come out at school. I'd told him that I was afraid he'd be beaten up if he came out in high school. He wanted to start a Gay-Straight Alliance in his school the coming fall. I said that I thought he was asking for trouble.

Lisa's response, in retrospect, was what I should have known myself. It made me think. It's what I know today. But when going through this, I didn't have the necessary perspective. I needed to stop worrying about everything. My son attended a nice school. Most of the kids there thought it was cool to have an openly gay friend. "I think Carl should do what he wants to do," she said.

II

Self-Help and Counselors

BOOKS ⌒

No sooner had carl come out to me, than i drove to a downtown bookstore, where I was certain I could remain anonymous, and picked up the one title on the shelf for parents with LGBT children. The book had originally been published in 1979 and had been revised twice. I was in serious undercover mode. I made sure I read it only in the evening after the boys were in bed. I stopped reading it when I came to the section that cited statistics from a 1959 survey of sexual activity amongst prison inmates. I cried, thinking my son was going to turn into a criminal. The other overarching theme of the book examined the question, "Did I do something that made my son gay?" This section left me thinking that it was my fault Carl was gay. Neither of these ideas was helpful. I'd like to have a read a book about ways to help my child come out instead of a book that pointed fingers and assigned blame. I stopped reading the book, got out of bed, went downstairs, and dropped it into the recycling box.

The same strategy has worked for me ever since, when I've received pamphlets from people who distribute information that claimed my child and I were sinners. I send them on their way and put their material in the recycling. Long ago I stopped feeling guilty. No one can make someone gay. It's not a choice.

COUNSELORS ⌒

Prior to learning about Parents, Families and Friends of Lesbians and Gays (pflag) support group meetings, I searched for basic information and guidance. Leonard and I went to see the same counselor we had met with about Carl's night terrors. We told her Carl was gay and were surprised when she confirmed that when she first met Carl she thought it was likely he was gay.

We wanted to know what had made her think this.

He had told her that *Moulin Rouge* was one of his favourite movies. She took this as a strong indicator. Leonard and I sat in her office, looking at each other, gob-smacked for a few seconds. She went on to explain the stereotype: many gay men like musicals. Her comment made me think maybe lgbt issues were not her area of expertise. Stereotypes are meaningless.

We have two sons. One son has dozens of pairs of brightly coloured shoes, keeps abreast of the latest clothing fashions, many of his closest friends have always been girls, and he was constantly frustrated with his roommates for not keeping the apartment neat and clean. The other is a competitive water polo player with a clear, booming voice and a firm handshake who dresses conservatively. Both of them were fans of *Moulin Rouge*. Which one is gay? Here's a hint: it's not the one with all the shoes. There's no guarantee a girl who is a perky cheerleader is straight. lgbt people are as diverse in the way they present themselves and what they do as the rest of the general population.

Although the counselor tried to be supportive, she wasn't aware of pflag nor did she recommend any books on parenting an lgbt child. The "*Moulin Rouge* strong indicator" comment put us off. We didn't return. Helping professionals such as counselors, psychologists, social workers, ministers, priests, rabbis, and imams may have expertise in individual and couples counseling, addictions, eating disorders, depression, sexual abuse, and therapy among many other specialties, but that doesn't mean they are competent, trained in, or in some cases even open to helpful discussion on lgbt issues. The counselor said something to us that didn't make sense. It's possible we weren't the problem and the real issue was she didn't have a clue what she was talking about.

LOOKING FOR HELP ⌐

WHILE CARL WAS ON exchange in Quebec, I called the Gay and Lesbian Community Centre of Edmonton (GLCCE) hoping to speak with someone who would provide me with basic information about where to go to get support. Instead of doing a Google search, I closed my office door and leafed through the phone book. I was paranoid about someone finding out I had called the gay and lesbian centre if my online activity was ever monitored. I found the number and waited a couple of more days. I finally found the courage and had a few spare minutes at work so I dialled the number. No one answered the phone. Instead, a recording came on advising office hours were from two p.m. to ten p.m. and requested callers leave a message so their call could be returned. I called every day for two weeks during those hours, desperate for someone to pick up the phone. No one answered and I didn't leave a message. I couldn't risk getting a return call at home because Paul still didn't know. And at work, even though only I had access to my phone messages, I felt I had to control when the conversation would happen if someone from the centre happened to call back.

The week Carl left for Quebec, Leonard and I were at the High Level Diner, a restaurant near campus. While standing in line to get in, I leafed through an issue of *SEE* Magazine, which is an alternative weekly arts and entertainment magazine. I found the QUEER category in the classifieds/listing section. As I read through the QUEER listings I found notices for a radio show, curling, volleyball and swim clubs, a choir, coming-out support groups, two listings for PFLAG (with no description of what the letters represented), the Edmonton Rainbow Business Association, and a notice for what I thought was a support group for parents with LGBT children.

When I read the words LGBT *parents*, I interpreted them in the same way as if I had read *choir parents* or *soccer parents*. It hadn't occurred to me to search the internet for "support groups for parents of gay kids" to see what was available in Edmonton. I was relieved to see the little classified ad. I tore out the page, put it in my purse, and put the magazine back on the rack — odd behaviour on my part, considering the magazines were available free-of-charge for anyone to take. A couple of days later, while Paul was out, I called the number. I was expecting a straight parent with an LGBT child. But Gerry, a gay man who had a straight son, was on the other end of the line. It turned out YMOU was a support group for gays and lesbians who had children — not a helpline for straight parents with gay children. Gerry listened as I cried. In between sobs I told him that my seventeen-year-old son was gay. I told him how I was worried about what his life is going to be like as a gay man in the world.

Gerry was patient. He said how there had been a big change in the last ten years. He was in his forties. When he was Carl's age he never would have predicted same-sex couples would be adopting children or getting married. In 2003 in Ontario same-sex marriages had already been performed for a year. He asked me how Leonard felt about having a gay son.

I told him that it wasn't an issue for him, except that we were both worried about everything. How was Carl going to tell his brother? What was going to happen at school if the kids find out? We didn't know how to tell our families. I had countless questions for Gerry. How would our friends and neighbours react? I couldn't help myself. The questions I'd been unable to articulate poured out of me. Carl was going off to university the following year, and I was worried about what was going to happen to him if he wound up with a homophobic roommate in residence. I was asking this poor man on the other end of the phone to gaze into a crystal ball and tell me what Carl's life was going to be like.

Gerry did just that. His most comforting insight was to advise that there would be some bumps along the road, but he thought Carl would have a good life. The single most important thing for Carl was that he had parents who supported him. He paused. "It sounds like you are doing a good job. I wish my parents would have had your reaction." Even though I was worried and paranoid about Carl's life as a gay man there was never a moment when my love for my son and my devotion to him faltered. Gerry went on to tell me that he had been married and had a son. He had a partner now, but was not out at work. His job was in the trades.

Misreading the parental support classified ad was the best mistake I made in those early months because it put me in touch with Gerry. I called him every few months, sometimes just to say hi and other times to get his opinion on PFLAG issues. We became good telephone friends, but hadn't laid eyes on each other. I invited him and his partner to meet me at work in the Students' Union Building for coffee. On a warm summer afternoon, two middle-aged men arrived dressed in golf shirts and walking shorts wearing matching Birkenstock sandals. The matching Birkenstocks made me smile. Gerry was one of my best supports. Although it was helpful for me to speak with parents who had gay kids, hearing first hand, lived experiences from a calm, thoughtful, middle-aged gay man helped ease me through those early months and years by slowly reducing my overwhelming fears. Gerry made me feel that we were all in this together. Both he and I were parents with children we loved and wanted the best for. Even if my experience was different from his, he accepted me and made me feel that I belonged, we were all part of the same human community.

The evening I first spoke with Gerry, I felt confident enough to call GLCCE, this time during office hours. Lawrence answered the phone. I had the identical conversation with Lawrence as I had had minutes before with Gerry. I cried yet again, and Lawrence listened. He gave me practically the same advice: there would be some challenges, but the most important thing for Carl was to have supportive parents. It felt so good to speak with these two men. I needed to speak with gay men who were honest about what might be ahead for Carl but, most importantly, I needed to hear them say they were happy with their own lives and that they thought my son would be happy as well.

Although it's been years since I last bumped into Gerry or Lawrence, I've since established many friendships with members of the LGBT community all over Canada and the United States. This wouldn't have happened had I not had a gay son. My new LGBT friends have supported me and shown so much care and concern for Carl. When we get together or talk on the phone, the first thing they ask is, "How's Carl doing?"

In order to make sense of what to do about Carl's sexuality, Leonard and I attended a few PFLAG meetings, which had been recommended to me when I called the gay and lesbian centre looking for information and help. Each time we went to a PFLAG meeting we lied to Paul about where we were going, saying that we had a reception at work. To honour one son's request that he be allowed to come out to his brother when he felt the time was right, we were driven to lie to the other son about attending the support group we needed. I felt guilty each time I lied to Paul. I waited until Paul was out of the house to have telephone conversations with Carl in Quebec when there was something I wanted to tell him about PFLAG.

Going to PFLAG meetings and my clandestine telephone conversations with Carl felt like I was engaged in an undercover operation. We parked the car at least a block away from the gay and lesbian centre. We looked over our shoulders to see if there was anyone around we recognized or needed to avoid. As we passed people on the street we made sure not to make eye contact and then quickly entered the building. To make matters worse, the PFLAG meeting facilitators introduced themselves using only their first names. Following the tone that was set by the facilitators, the parents used their first names only. I couldn't understand why. Was being there shameful, potentially dangerous, or morally wrong? Although the overall experience of PFLAG meetings was helpful, the imposed anonymity sometimes made me feel like I was guilty of having a gay kid.

The hiding, secrecy, paranoia, and fear around homosexuality for so many in my generation are based on our upbringing and experiences during a deeply homophobic time in North American history. When I was in high school in the late 1960s and early seventies there were a couple of boys we all knew were gay. Sadly, these boys took a lot of teasing and were often referred to as "fairies." In a high school of four hundred students, there had to be at least thirty LGBT students, based on the most frequently published statistics that say eight to twelve percent of the population is gay. Some articles cite homosexuality and same-sex attraction in the general population as low as two percent and other research has it at twenty-six. Where were all the gay kids? They were all closeted. Most likely none of them were out to themselves, never mind anyone else at school. Homosexuality was decriminalized in Canada in 1969, one year after I started high school. Until then, people could be charged and jailed for having consensual sex with a same-sex partner.

After Carl came home from the exchange in Quebec, he continued to put off coming out to Paul. He assured me he was going to talk to his brother. As the days and weeks went by he continued to stall.

He made up excuses. "I'll tell him on the weekend. Paul's got exams now."

He did everything possible to avoid the conversation. "Can't do it now, I've got a rehearsal at school tonight."

I tried to be patient, agreeing that it wasn't a good idea to rush the discussion. I encouraged Carl to talk to Paul when he was ready. I had to be sympathetic to both my sons. "I know it's difficult for you, but Paul needs to know. He can't be the only person in this family who doesn't know."

As the weeks turned into months, I could see Carl was making it harder for himself than necessary. I knew Paul would react fine when Carl told him. Paul was the most loyal person I knew. I didn't understand what Carl was so worried about. I didn't understand why he was avoiding telling his brother. But I didn't want to have a battle with him about his timing.

By the end of the school year, I found myself faced with eight weeks of summer vacation with two teenage boys knocking around the house between summer camps and trips. Leonard and I had a PFLAG meeting to go to that first week and I was fed up with lying to Paul about where we were going. I found a moment when both boys were in the house together, doing nothing, when neither of them had plans to go out. Paul was playing computer games in another room. Carl was in the kitchen standing in front of the open fridge. I gently but firmly told Carl it was time. "Dad and I have a PFLAG meeting tonight and we're not going to lie to Paul any longer about where we're going. You have to tell him now." Carl needed the push. There was no argument or debate. He closed the fridge, turned around, went into the den, told his brother he was gay, and was back in the kitchen thirty seconds later.

"How did it go?"

"He told me it was fine and not to go all Liberace on him. Then he went back to the computer game. I was kind of hoping to talk about it some more with him but I'm glad it's over."

"He's fourteen years old, he's doing the best he can."

Ten years later Carl would say he was happy that day. His disclosure was nothing to Paul. Telling him didn't change a thing between them. Carl had stalled and procrastinated because he was worried Paul wouldn't accept him or would react badly.

After Carl came out to Paul, he was ready to come out to everyone. A girl Carl knew from choir happened to be sitting beside him at a concert our family was attending. During intermission, though not intending to eavesdrop, I overheard her ask, "Do you have a girlfriend?" I bit my bottom lip, closed my eyes, and thought, Oh, no. Here we go. How is he going to answer this? Then, I deliberately listened to the next part of their conversation.

"No."

She prodded, "Everyone has a girlfriend."

Carl paused, turned his head to make eye contact with her and cautiously said, "Not everyone. I'm gay."

"Oh, cool," she chirped and went on talking about her summer plans.

I turned to Leonard and whispered, "He just told her he was gay and she said it was cool." This kind of low-key reaction was proving to be the norm as Carl continued to come out that summer. He wanted people to accept him for who he was and not for who they thought he was. And if the question arose, Leonard and I were to tell anyone who asked that our son was gay.

While his father and I initially worried about Carl being bullied and harassed at school, we got the impression that for many of the kids it was indeed cool to have an openly gay friend. How times had changed.

But not everything was perfect. There was discord. Paul quickly felt Carl talked about being gay all of the time. It was too much. He wanted Carl to stop talking about it because it didn't matter to him and his friends. This hurt Carl.

I explained that Paul and his friends were thirteen- and fourteen-year-old boys who were doing the best they could for their age. Maybe Carl could cool it when he was around them.

RIGHT AFTER CARL CAME out to Paul, I called my mom and sister and also spoke with my closest friends. I called my friend, Judy, who lived a block away, telling her that I needed to come over.

I was already crying as she and I walked into their home office and closed the door. Judy had prepared for the worst — which, coming from our house, could well mean another cancer diagnosis. Years afterwards, Judy told me that she was so relieved to hear that my news wasn't anything serious. Judy and her husband Craig first told Sarah, their eldest daughter, who was in high school. They had a few discussions about how and when they were going to tell Claire, their twelve-year-old daughter. Their girls and our boys had known each other their entire lives; they were like family. For a few days Judy and Craig carefully reviewed what they were going to say to Claire so she would understand what they were talking about. They had anticipated all the questions and were ready for an uncomfortable conversation.

The right day and time arrived. When her parents told her that they had something important to talk to her about, tiny, fiercely competitive Claire — an A-student and accomplished athlete with straight blond hair she kept out of her eyes with a barrette — braced herself for the worst. "Carl is gay," they said. Claire waited for them to get to whatever the important thing was they needed to talk about. There had to be something else because her mom and dad were so serious. Judy and Craig immediately realized Carl being gay really wasn't an issue for Claire. No further explanation or discussion was required. Claire's response was to ask if the conversation was over, she had other things to do.

Paul once talked about how he would have to tell his children their Uncle Carl was gay. I realized that it was likely he would never need to explain. His children would grow up knowing their uncle as he was. Since each day of children's lives is made up of learning new things, Paul's kids would know this is what Uncle Carl's family and life looks like, no explanation required. This will be normal for them. I thought of that earlier conversation I'd had with Lisa.

III

Out to Family

Just as carl had spent months trying to figure out how to come out to the three of us, I too worried about how things would go with my mom and sister when I told them the news. A few days after Carl came out to Paul, my sister and I spent a weekend together at a sports tournament one of her kids was playing in. We lived several hundred kilometres apart and the tournament was being held in a location less than three hours' drive from Edmonton. We sat in the bleachers, watched every game, ate together, and shared a motel room — particularly memorable as it had a bare light bulb hanging on a cord from the ceiling. We howled with laughter as we tried not to touch any of the sticky surfaces in the room and didn't dare walk around in bare feet on a carpet that had a thin layer of translucent grey sediment and deposits of dead bugs in the corners. There were many perfect opportunities for me to tell my sister about my son's declaration, but I couldn't get a word out. I was afraid of how she would react. I went to the tournament because I knew we would have time to talk, alone with just the two of us. A day and a half later I got into my car to drive home without having told her.

A few days after the tournament, feeling that I couldn't avoid the conversation any longer, I called her. She picked up the phone. We talked while she organized her Tupperware drawer. I bared my soul. "This won't be a problem for my family," she said as she continued sorting and stacking plastic food containers.

I was surprised. She was so blasé about my disclosure. I told her I would be calling our mother in a couple of days and asked her not to mention the news if they spoke. She agreed.

That was it. The conversation was over. I had hoped to have a more in-depth conversation. The exchange left me feeling the same way Carl said he felt when he told Paul. The difference here was my sister was a forty-four-year-old mother whose kids were the same age as mine.

My sister lived in my hometown, across the alley from our mother. I felt she needed a few days to process what I'd revealed before I told our mother. My thinking was that once she had processed the knowledge that her nephew was gay, my sister would be able to help Mom, who was eighty-two. I was certain my mother would be shocked.

Three days later, I called my mother. As the phone rang I started to choke up. When she answered, I couldn't speak. Tears streamed down my face. My mom heard my muffled sobs and sniffles. She waited and gently asked what was wrong. I remained speechless. In almost a whisper she repeated herself. By now she, too, was crying. "Tell me," she pleaded softly.

"Carl's gay," I said sobbing.

"That's it?" she replied. "That's all? That's not a problem! He's not sick, there's nothing wrong. They told me my brother Fred was gay. This is not a problem."

It never would be a problem for her.

This was exactly what I needed to hear from my mother. She had the same response I'd had when Carl came to my office. On that day, my son was sad and needed to hear flat-out reassurances that things were going to be fine. My mother did the same thing the day I called. Her daughter was sad, so she delivered the same message on cue with unflinching conviction: everything was going to be okay.

A month later, my mother came to visit. I asked her how she felt about her grandson being gay.

She said that she had cried for three days, but that now she was all right. She wanted to talk to Carl privately, though.

I found Carl and sent him into the kitchen so see his Baba. She told him that it was all right that he was gay, but she didn't want him to get AIDS and die.

This, I realized, was the 2004 version of the sex talk my mother had given my sister and me in the sixties and seventies when she preached that she didn't want us to get pregnant and have a baby.

My mother, the boy's Baba, was born in Saskatchewan. She lived there her entire life. She was taken out of school to work on her parent's farm when she was in grade eight. At nineteen she married my father, a farm boy. They ran a small mixed farm for twenty-five years, then moved to town when I was ten. My father continued to hobby farm until his accidental death at the age of sixty-three, when a bale loader crushed him.

Baba was the second youngest of thirteen children; her brother Fred, my gay uncle, was the second eldest. My grandfather was a widower with five children when he married his second wife, my grandmother, with whom he had eight more children. Eleven of the thirteen children lived to adulthood. Through my aunts, uncles, and cousins we were part of a large, loving, and supportive extended family. There were dozens of weddings, funerals, baptisms, church holy days, business successes and failures, alcoholism, car accidents, and countless joyful reunions and tearful farewells at the Saskatoon train station and airport. I have a cousin whose son was a professional golfer, another cousin belongs to a motorcycle gang, one cousin has a swimming pool, and another cousin has been in jail. I met him once. He had missing teeth. All of my cousins on my mother's side of the family were older than me. Some were older than my mother. Between these families and their extended families a great deal of living happened. There was no shortage of variety. There wasn't much that would surprise my mother.

It took my husband several months longer than me to tell his family Carl was gay. He rationalized that he didn't want to do it over the phone. His parents and one sister lived in Florida, and another sister lived in Michigan. He travelled to Florida at least a couple of times a year, but it was going to be a while before he would see his sister in Michigan. I worried that he was trying to avoid the conversations. I encouraged and pressured him to get it over with.

I told him it was easier over the phone. This is how I had told my sister and my mother. If anyone had a problem with the news, he won't have to deal with it in person. I was concerned that it might well be a few years before all five of his family were in the same place at one time.

He defended himself with honesty, saying that it was natural to avoid things because they're hard.

After months of stalling, he finally called. His mother, Omi, sweetly responded, "We have this in the family, you know," and quickly got his father, Grandpa, on the phone.

Without hesitation, my father-in-law said that it was good that Carl could be himself. His Uncle Jerry had had to hide his whole life. It was hard for him. Uncle Jerry Burke was my husband's great uncle, Carl and Paul's great-great uncle. He had been a professional musician in the Lawrence Welk Band. When Leonard and I got married in 1980, my father-in-law, who was Uncle Jerry's favourite nephew, was still receiving small royalty cheques from the Lawrence Welk Band for records Uncle Jerry had performed on. My father and mother-in-law said everyone knew Uncle Jerry and Ray, the man he lived with in Santa Monica, who was an engineer at Lockheed, were not just roommates, but no one talked about it. It was relief to have the conversations with our parents over with, especially since the conversations had gone well.

Leonard's mother was born in Germany in 1919 and grew up in Berlin. As a child she witnessed her Jewish friends move away or disappear. She and her mother fled Berlin when the Russians invaded at the end of World War II. Because she and her sister were fluent in English, they both worked for the American Armed Forces during the occupation of Berlin after the War. In addition to their salaries, the German employees received a noonday meal from the Americans. After years of starvation, having a regular meal everyday was like a gift from God. My mother-in-law worshipped Americans for the rest of her life. At work she met a young Jewish American serviceman whom she married. They went back to the US and lived in New York, but the marriage quickly ended. She moved to Milwaukee, where there was a large German population, to be with her sister, who had also married an American serviceman, but he was of German descent. Milwaukee has a suburb called New Berlin pronounced New BER-lin with a drawn-out accent on the first syllable. In Milwaukee she met and married Leonard's father, a former US Marine who had been stationed in Pearl Harbor during the War only a year after the bombings.

My father-in-law had jet-black hair until he turned eighty. He wished he had had at least some grey because no one believed he didn't colour his hair. He loved the Three Stooges, told the same corny jokes his entire life, and had his own vocabulary. Babies and small children were "gooies" — as in sticky. An egg was a "Palmorine" — Herman Palmorine was the old farmer who had delivered eggs when he was a child. My mother-in-law's car was "the whoopee" — regardless of the make or model. A screwdriver was a "Colorado" — for reasons nobody could determine. The list went on and on.

Omi had lived through the horrors of Nazi Germany and World War II. Grandpa had lived through the Depression and drought in South Dakota in the 1930s. Like my mother, they were devoted parents and grandparents who loved and supported their children and their families.

Leonard called his sisters, Lynne and Diane, right after he spoke with his parents. The conversations went smoothly. Both sisters took the information in stride. Diane later said that the next time she got together with her parents, they shared that Leonard had called and that they all knew. Their father felt bad because life would be harder for Carl. He was concerned for his grandson. Their mother had a history of tolerance, so this information meant very little to her. She loved her grandson. There was no gnashing of teeth. This was not going to be a major family talking point.

Lynne, Leonard's other sister, said their father had confided in her that he had suspected his grandson was gay. This explained why my father and mother in-law didn't flinch when Leonard told them Carl was gay. That's why my father-in-law said it was good Carl could be himself. He already knew. Lynne added that their mother wanted to have Carl down to Florida. She wanted him to know for sure they were fine with this news. As a grade twelve graduation gift, Carl spent a week with Omi and Grandpa in St. Petersburg, Florida over the Christmas break.

I've had many conversations with parents, LGBT youth, and adults who agonize about coming out to grandparents. They worry that their grandparents are old, religious, or members of any number of ethnic groups. Each individual knows his or her own circumstances best but age, religion, and ethnic origin are not necessarily reliable predictors of responses to such information. I reassure such people by reminding them that their grandparents have lived a very long time and have probably seen or been part of many changes in their lifetime. It's possible long ago they had already dealt with something similar with other relatives or friends. Kindness, the way people behave and conduct themselves, and the comments they make might be better indicators. But even then, there's really no way of knowing for certain how things will go, whether for good or bad. I saw this with one of Carl's most supportive teachers when her son came out — she, like me, was shaken by the unexpected news and reacted with disbelief and fear.

Although Carl's grandparents stood by us, predictably not all our relatives accepted having an openly gay family member with grace and sensitivity. One individual — well known for his sexist, ethnic, and homophobic insults — kept himself in check for a few years. Eventually, he slowly resumed making homophobic comments. Our contact over the years had been limited mostly to periodic telephone conversations. I happened to call one evening during a civic election campaign and he answered the phone. When I asked him how his current mayor was, he answered that he was a fag. He didn't offer much else. Another time, he described the paint job on his neighbours' boat as "gay." At an anniversary party a group was debating the merits of retired Edmonton Oilers hockey players. He added comments like "He's got a mullet. He's a fairy." His sister touched his arm and laughingly said, "Don't," in a feeble attempt to get him to stop. When he made a third homophobic comment during the banquet, his wife tapped him on the shoulder, frowned and gently said, "Okay, stop." She used the same tone of voice she would use to correct a child for dropping Cheerios one-by-one off a highchair tray. Leonard and Paul's eyes were fixed on me, waiting for me to say something.

I tilted my head to the side and back, and leaned in. A couple of seconds passed as I glared at him across the table. Through clenched teeth I ordered, "Can you stop saying those things."

"Whaaat, I don't mean nothin'," he said, meeting my glare straight on.

Trying to diminish my reaction, another guest chastised me, saying he hadn't meant anything bad. He was free to say what he wanted. The rest of table chimed in, advising me to let it go, to forget about it. Some of them tried to dismiss my reaction so they wouldn't have to deal with his wrath later, while others genuinely believed he had the right to say whatever he felt like saying. The group scolded me for speaking up, saying I was oversensitive and making an issue out of nothing. No one said a word to him. He didn't apologize, nor did he try to defend himself. Leonard, Paul, and I should have got up and left, but we didn't because I was afraid to upset more people than I already had. We politely finished the rest of our meal even though we didn't feel like eating. In silence we sat through a couple of toasts and speeches, leaving after what felt like an eternity.

I didn't tell Carl about the homophobic remarks because I didn't want to hurt him, convincing myself he didn't need to know. After all, he was living in Toronto, thousands of kilometres away, and he wouldn't be seeing those relatives. I thought I could protect him. Not long after this unpleasant event, the same relative and his family went to Ontario for their friends' daughter's wedding. While there, they invited Carl to join them for dinner. Again, I consciously chose not to say a word to Carl about what had gone on at the anniversary party. By doing this I betrayed my child and ended up protecting someone who was unworthy of any form of grace.

Three months later, when I was overwhelmed with guilt, I told Carl about the homophobic comments. He was angry with me. Had he known about the earlier comments and the dinner exchange, he likely would have reacted differently to the invitation and perhaps interacted differently with this particular individual. "At the very least," Carl said, "if I'd known about what had gone on, it would have informed my decision to spend time with them."

For the last several years I've had no contact with this family. I don't have to endure offensive comments, even when the comments originate from relatives. Friends, counselors, and all sorts of wise individuals advise people to stop doing the things that hurt them. I stopped subjecting myself to him. I had been silent and had listened to his insults long enough. Difficult as it was to admit, I felt much better knowing I would no longer have any association with him. I stopped calling and have avoided contact ever since.

Part Two

I

The GSA

During his final year of high school Carl began the process of starting a gay/straight alliance (GSA) student support group. Strathcona High School had a history of athletic excellence in swimming, track and field, cross-country, and football. In 2004 the track team had won thirty-one consecutive city track and field championships, twenty-five consecutive city championships for the cross-country team, and eighteen consecutive city championships for the swim team. The football team had won four consecutive city championships and was provincial champion in 2001 and 2002. That same year the swim team was made up of two hundred and fifty students and it felt like all fourteen hundred students were on the track team. At Strathcona there was an athletics culture where full school participation was encouraged and everyone was welcomed.

For months Carl and I had argued about his plan to come out and his plan to start the GSA. My position was simple. Only over my dead body was Carl going to go out on this thin limb. I wanted him to keep quiet, keep his head down, and finish high school without creating problems for himself.

He pleaded that the hallways at Strathcona were full of students who had a secret they couldn't tell anyone. This was a terrible burden. The casual homophobia he and the other students endured almost constantly was too much to bear when feeling alone. A GSA would give gay students a safe space at school, at lunchtime, one day a week. Students in the club would get to meet other students who understood what they were going through and accept them just the way they are.

It took too long for me to understand what my son was talking about, because I was worried about bullying. I remembered the relentless teasing my high school classmates had endured and I wanted to protect my child from similar abuse and harassment. I also remembered an earlier experience in my son's life.

When Carl was in grade six, Larry, his classmate since kindergarten, regularly shoved him into the wall whenever they passed each other in the hallway. I went to Larry's house to have a mom-to-mom conversation. I rang the doorbell and was invited inside. I got right to the point. "I need to talk to you about what Larry is doing to Carl at school. Every time Larry and Carl walk by each other, Larry shoves Carl into the wall."

"I know he does that, he hates Carl."

Her statement stunned me. "Why does he hate Carl?"

"Larry talks about how much he hates Carl all the time to his older brother."

I waited to hear why Larry hated Carl. I waited for an apology. I waited for Larry's mother to tell me that she had tried everything she could think of to get him to stop. I expected her to be shocked by what I said, or to deny her child was bullying my child. But none of this happened. Instead I got the impression it hadn't occurred to her that she could have any impact on a twelve-year-old's behaviour. The conversation was pointless and a waste of time. As I left I made a final request. "Do you think you could tell Larry to stop shoving Carl?"

"Won't do any good, he hates Carl."

I went to see the school principal, who set up a meeting. Carl, his teacher, the school principal, Leonard, and I sat around a child-sized table, on child-sized chairs in the elementary school library. Larry and his mother were not there. I recounted what had gone on with Larry and Carl, and my conversation with Larry's mother.

"Why didn't you tell me earlier, Carl?" was the first thing that came out of the principal's mouth. Twelve-year-old Carl, in a room with four adults, defended himself saying he thought Larry would stop. Carl, the victim, was made to feel like he had done something wrong by not seeking help sooner. The principal promised to speak with Larry and asked Carl to report back to him if the shoving continued. The shoving stopped. Although Carl had always been tall for his age, a growth spurt a year later made him one of the tallest kids in junior high and bullying was never an issue after that.

No matter my son's height, I worried about what grade twelve Larry, who was still a classmate in high school, and like-minded others would do when they found out Carl was gay. Would they engage in the high school version of shoving? I didn't want Carl to create additional problems for himself. We debated his coming out and GSA plans many, many times. I begged him not to come out at school, not to set up a GSA. He pleaded that he had to. The heated discussions inevitably turned into arguments. "High school kids are immature. You're asking for trouble. Can't you wait until you're in university? I know what I'm talking about!"

"I think I have a better idea of what high school's like now than you do Mom. If I don't set up a GSA, no one else will." Carl wouldn't give up and eventually wore me down. It helped to learn that all the friends he came out to during the summer and the first couple months of school in the fall were completely supportive and accepting.

At the end of October in his final year of high school, Carl met with his high school principal to get permission to start a GSA. The principal said she had to speak with her staff and other principals. There was no word from her for weeks. A few days before the Christmas break, the principal asked Carl to prepare a proposal outlining his rationale for a GSA at Strathcona High School. He worked on the proposal and submitted it to the principal right after the break.

Proposal for the Creation of a
Gay–Straight Student Alliance at Strathcona High School
BY CARL SWANSON
JANUARY 6, 2004

A year and a half ago, I realized that I was gay. Though now I feel comfortable with both my life and who I am, at that time I felt incredibly alone and alienated, as do all youth and adults who discover that their sexuality is anything but heterosexual. Though I had many friends and a close family, I did not know anyone else my age who was going through the same thing I was, much less anyone whom I could talk to about what I was going through. At this time, all I wanted was to meet someone that truly understood how I felt; someone who knew what it was like to be a gay teenager or who would be supportive of my identity.

High school aged teenagers spend their time in three different places: at home, with their friends, and at school. There was certainly no easy way for me to find a visibly supportive person at school. I had to look outside of school, a place where I spend eight hours of every weekday, in order to find a group of people who were going through the same thing I was. This group was Youth Understanding Youth, an outreach program at the Gay and Lesbian Community Centre of Edmonton. Had there been an opportunity for me to meet other lesbian, gay, bisexual or transgender youth at Scona, I would not have had to go downtown, by myself, to an unfamiliar office building full of people who I had never met before. I should have been able to find support at my school. I would have given anything to see a face I recognized. Furthermore, a great many youth would be too intimidated to get out of their house, go to a strange place, and meet strange people when they are already dealing with a great deal of emotional pressure.

Fortunately for me, meeting other gay youth and supportive adults was a wonderful experience. I came home afterwards feeling the best I had in nearly a year. Many students at Scona are currently going through the same feelings of alienation that I went through, and it is essential that they have a safe and caring place to go where they can meet other people like themselves. This is precisely why Strathcona High school needs a Gay–Straight Student Alliance (GSA). A GSA will create a space where lesbian, gay, bisexual, trans-gender, questioning and straight students can go to hang out, relax, and support each other. A sense of community, a sense that they are not alone, is incredibly important to any youth who may be beginning to understand their identity. Being a teenager is difficult enough, now imagine feeling like you have no one to turn to, no place to really feel like you can be yourself. Scona was this place for me.

An active GSA will be of great benefit to all the students and teachers at Strathcona. GSAS already exist all over the world, and in a handful of high schools in Alberta. Just the simple presence of such a club will send a message to students that you are safe to be yourself at Scona. The hallways at Scona are full of students who have a secret they can't tell anyone. This is a terrible burden, and added to the casual homophobia that these students encounter almost constantly, whether perceived or real, can become too much to bear. Students who choose to be involved in the club will get to meet other students who understand what they are going through and accept them for whom they are. And most importantly, students at Scona will realize that they go to a wonderfully diverse and accepting school where diversity is something embraced, not feared.

POTENTIAL ACTIVITIES
— Weekly meetings: A chance for students to meet and hang out with other understanding students and supportive teacher facilitators
— Group Discussions (on topics such as coming out and heterosexism)
— Q&A Day
— Planning Meetings
— Movie Nights
— Guest Speakers (politicians, PFLAG, community leaders)
— Barbeques (possibly with other Edmonton GSAS)
— Outdoor Activities
— Multicultural Events/Pride Week Celebrations
— Day of Awareness (AIDS, youth suicide, community & history (Stonewall) etc.)

Being a teenager is hard enough without having to hide who you are. It would be a tremendous step forward if Strathcona High School became one of the leading high schools that have chosen to help out some of the most neglected, forgotten, and abused youth in our society. I hope that we create a *Gay–Straight Student Alliance* at Strathcona, so no one has to hide anymore.

The principal said she had to take the proposal to the Edmonton Public School Board. A few days later, she told Carl he couldn't start a new club because it would conflict with the semester's final exams.

It had taken Carl months to change my mind and now it was taking months for him to get permission at school. The principal's hesitation was understandable, I rationalized. This was her first year at Strathcona. We knew what she was being asked to do was precedent-setting in the public school system, but she was treating it like delicate surgery. I had the feeling the principal was stalling, so I made an appointment with her to find out what was going on. Carl's coming out had added a new dimension to our family dynamics. LGBT social justice issues now directly affected us. We switched from simply thinking of ourselves as socially conscious to actually becoming vocal public advocates for equal treatment and basic human rights for the LGBT community. In less than a year I had gone from parking my car around the corner when Leonard and I attended PFLAG meetings to demanding that my son have the right to form a GSA in Edmonton's oldest public high school.

"I'm responsible for the safety of all the students," the principal said. "I'm uneasy with Carl's plan for the GSA." She got up and walked over to a storage cabinet beside her desk. To my horror, she showed me a Ku Klux Klan costume she had confiscated. "One of the students wore this to school on Halloween last fall." The principal was a middle-aged black woman.

She was right, she did have a responsibility to protect all the students. She didn't want to single out the LGBT students, but avoiding the creation of a GSA would not make life better for them. "The LGBT kids need evidence they are being supported and protected. You've got to at least let him try to make the club work," I replied.

I set up a meeting with the principal and Kris Wells, a U of A graduate student who was working on LGBT issues in schools and also the coordinator of a youth drop-in at the gay and lesbian centre. Kris, a former teacher and young man in his thirties, explained the importance of the GSA and the impact her leadership and support of the club would have within Edmonton public schools. The meeting with Kris helped persuade the principal to allow the formation of the club.

It took four months from the initial conversation with his principal in October before, in late February 2004, Carl was given permission to schedule the first lunchtime GSA meeting. With just over four months of school left in his graduating year it was barely adequate time to establish a new club. He was told that because the school was concerned for the safety of the students he was not allowed to put up any posters, nor was he allowed to include the notice in the daily announcements. Students were somehow supposed to know when and where the meeting was taking place. Given the principal's concern for student safety, how safe was it for Carl, and the handful of friends he had helping him, to go around telling other students about the meeting?

I could see Carl was disheartened when he came home after the first meeting.

"How'd it go today?" I asked, trying to be upbeat.

"Only six students and five teachers showed up."

"What! That's actually great, Carl," I said, my mood switching to genuine enthusiasm. "With that many teachers it means there's solid school support. You don't have to worry, the club's here to stay."

Within two weeks the meetings were part of the daily announcements. The GSA students named the group Diversity Club, and by the next fall the Diversity Club had a sign-up table in the school gym on Clubs Day, along with all other school clubs. The following spring the Diversity Club was part of the Pep Rally when all clubs and teams march across the stage in front of the entire school.

Of the fourteen hundred students in his school, Carl estimated there were one hundred LGBT kids. He said, "If I feel like I need to be with people who know what it's like to be gay, there have to be other students who feel the same way. School has to be a safe place for all of us and also a place where we can meet others who are gay. It's not enough to be out to straight people." From his experience at the youth drop-in, he knew there were many students whose families' didn't support them and that it was likely there were students in every classroom who were being teased, bullied, or harassed because of their sexual orientation.

I ran into one of Carl's teachers while waiting for a subway train and we got talking about the GSA. Carl and I had no idea to what length the principal and teachers had gone to be prepared for the creation of the club. The teacher informed me that the first year of the GSA the teachers' support was in no way random. They were all on the alert for the first few months. On the day of the first meeting, two students on the football team had come by the classroom intending to intimidate the students going into the room and to disrupt the meeting inside. He said the teachers knew which of them needed to be near the door. The teacher stationed at the classroom door had a reputation for being one of the toughest no-nonsense on staff. She could handle predictably unpredictable situations requiring immediate disciplinary action. Although she never had Carl in her class, she was there because the GSA was a student initiative that needed school-wide support. She brought the football players to the principal's office where they met with their coach, who was also one of two vice-principals. The boys were suspended from the football team, setting the tone for the existence of the club for the rest of the year. It was a serious step to throw players off the most celebrated high school football team in the city. But there was no question that day: there would be zero tolerance for any kind of bullying and harassment. The mistreatment of the GSA students would not be overlooked for the good of the school football team.

At the end of grade twelve Carl received a Top 20 under 20 Scholarship in a nationwide competition. A large part of his nomination was based on his creation of the Diversity Club. That year, two of the Top 20 winners had started GSAS in their high schools. Coincidentally, both GSAS were in Alberta. This was groundbreaking in 2004. There were four GSAS in Edmonton, one of which was at a Catholic high school and was officially underground since Catholic schools did not allow GSAS. The Top 20 winners received a small scholarship and were flown to Toronto for three days of tours, dinners, and mentorship in the middle of June final exams. Carl had to write one of his provincial finals while in Toronto. Graduating Alberta students' final grades were based on standardized provincial exams worth fifty percent of their final mark. While in Toronto, the group stayed in Chestnut, the residence Carl eventually lived in for his first two years at U of T. It was a great introduction to the university and Toronto. The few days he spent in Toronto as a Top 20 winner helped him decide U of T was the campus for him.

TEACHERS ⤳

TEACHERS WERE AN IMPORTANT part of my children's lives. Many were exemplary educators and fine, caring human beings. When Carl was having night terrors in grade ten, we asked his teachers if they saw any problems in school. After Carl started the GSA, his grade ten math teacher said, "I thought it was likely he was gay when you talked to me about the night terrors." Among the particularly supportive group of teachers, one had lost a brother to AIDS and another had a gay stepson.

Years later, one of the teachers called me. Her voice was barely louder than a whisper. She needed to talk to someone who knew how she felt. One of her sons had just come out to her.

In between long pauses she forced herself to speak. She had no idea she would feel this way. She was lost.

He had left his wife and his young family. This teacher was worried her son would move to another city, away from his children. She didn't know what to do. She was in shock.

When Carl started the GSA, she had been one of the strongest and most outspoken supporters of the club. On the phone, she said, "It was easy to be helpful and to support Carl and your family because it was the right thing to do." She had taught and guided thousands of kids and had dealt with almost as many parents. She comforted and reassured my family when we needed it. Now it was my turn to support her. Her son's disclosure was the same sort of shock to her as Carl's had been to me. Even though he was a grown man with a family, as a teacher she had first-hand experience with many of the struggles and obstacles that lay ahead for him and his family.

I told Carl's teacher that I understood she was close to her daughter-in-law. Their relationship didn't need to change. Her grandchildren would always be part of her life. But she had to make sure her son knew he still had her love and support.

"Taking this big step took a lot of strength for him," I said. I cautioned her that it would take a while for things to get sorted out. But because Carl had the conviction to start the GSA while he was still in high school, he did manage to create an opening for teachers who had LGBT family members or who themselves were LGBT to come out as well, if only to our family and a few others at school.

A few years later, when we were just getting involved with the local LGBT community, Leonard and I volunteered to be security chaperones at the Pride Week all-ages wrap-up dance. The dance was held off downtown in the Polish Hall. The place was packed and everyone was having fun. Rainbow-coloured lights flashed and the music blared as eight hundred people danced. Conversation was only possible downstairs, where the music was a little less deafeningly loud.

There were many friends and familiar faces in the crowd that night. Leonard and I were dancing when I glanced over and right beside me on the dance floor was one of Carl and Paul's former teachers dancing with his partner. It took a few seconds before I could place him. I smiled and asked him what he was doing at the dance.

With an even bigger smile he responded to me with the same question. We caught up as best we could between tunes. I found Carl on the dance floor and motioned for him to follow me. At first glance Carl didn't recognize the man. He studied his former teacher's face for a few seconds before realizing who he was — it was a perfect surprise. He was one of my boys' favourite teachers and it was wonderful to find out he was gay.

Ten years after Carl started the GSA, our son Paul, who was then twenty-four years old, attended the Pride Parade with his girlfriend Danni. She volunteered as a parade marshal. At home after the parade, Paul told us that he had been very emotional. There were over fifty Edmonton Public School Board trustees and staff dressed in purple Pride T-shirts, marching with a banner in the parade. This was quite a contrast from when Carl tried to get the GSA off the ground. Ten years later, EPSB was one of the largest groups participating in the Pride Parade. Their demonstration of their support is so important for students and parents alike. It makes a difference when people see elected trustees and high profile civic leaders walking side-by-side with the LGBT groups.

PRENTICE BILL 10 ᕬ

IN DECEMBER 2014, LESS than six months after the Pride Parade, the Alberta Government prepared to take a step backwards when they introduced Bill 10 in the legislature for debate. Previous legislation allowed parents to remove their children from the classroom when sexual orientation was being discussed. Opposition parties had brought forward several private members' bills in the hope of engendering meaningful debate and a vote that would ensure equality for the LGBT community in areas of human rights, the Alberta Marriage Act, and give students the right to form GSAs in publicly funded schools. The original version of Bill 10 stated if students were denied the right to form a GSA their recourse was to take their case to a court of law. A huge public outcry pointed out it would be impossible for junior high and high school students to have the financial resources necessary to hire legal counsel to pursue this issue through the judicial system. No one mentioned the process could take years and students would graduate before their cases were resolved. A couple of days after the first draft of the bill was brought forward, the Conservative government amended Bill 10 so that appeals could be made to the Minister of Education, who would in turn intervene on behalf of the students. The Bill was amended to allow students to form a GSA and meet outside of school property. The following day, hundreds of Albertans, who supported GSAs in schools, held a protest rally outside the Legislature. The Premier pulled Bill 10, saying the debate was being suspended to allow for further consultation; it would be reintroduced in the winter sitting.

I emailed Premier Jim Prentice and Sandra Jansen, the Member of the Legislative Assembly who proposed Bill 10, offering to help them "create better informed legislation." I said I could provide perspective and experience on the real world issues surrounding the creation of a GSA as it had become clear to me that there was a gap in their understanding of how the formation of a GSA in a school really worked.

At noon the next day MLA Jansen called to invite me to be part of an informal advisory group she was putting together in preparation to bring the bill back into the Legislature. I agreed to take part in the group, but did not hear back from Ms. Jansen.

During the following two months, parents who supported their teenaged LGBT children held town hall meetings, lobbied the government, and wrote letters to the editors of their newspapers. I wrote an opinion piece, which appeared in the *Edmonton Journal* on February 13, 2015. The difference this time was that parents were leading the public outcry — it wasn't left to LGBT activists. Hundreds of parents with their children at their side, along with LGBT activists and a handful of Liberal and New Democratic Party MLAs from around the province, forced the governing Conservative Party to change the original version of Bill 10. The topic transformed from being regarded as background noise during question period in the Legislature to a matter of fundamental human rights reform. The Minister of Education eventually visited schools with GSAs where he spoke with kids at GSA meetings. The students told the Minister they endured relentless daily teasing and bullying. They spoke about their fear of being thrown out of their homes if they were outed to their parents. Some talked about having suicidal thoughts. The students pointed out how meaningful it was to them to feel supported by their school by allowing the GSA to meet once a week. On March 10, 2015, after months of stalling, the government brought forward a fully amended Bill 10, which allowed GSAs in all private, public, and charter schools where their formation was requested. The same amendment added sexual orientation, sex, gender identity, and gender expression to the Alberta Bill of Rights; these were now protected by law from discrimination.

Alberta's population topped four million in 2014. There were over two thousand schools in the province. Only ninety-six were on record as having a GSA.

II

I Wish I Had Told You

BECAUSE CARL HAD GOOD GRADES, WAS ON THE STUDENTS' UNION EXECUTIVE and the swim team, and had started the GSA, he applied for and was awarded several scholarships. A reporter from the *Edmonton Journal* focused on the establishment of the GSA when she interviewed Carl about receiving a Canada Millennium Scholarship. At the end of the interview he allowed her to use his full name in the article. Three days later, the newspaper article appeared with Carl's name in the first sentence.

Our family was out. I was sure we were in deep trouble. Everyone in our neighbourhood read the *Edmonton Journal*. Everyone at work read it. I tormented myself. I was certain kids would throw eggs at our house, maybe worse. I wondered if Paul would get beat up at school. I fretted, irrationally, speculating I might lose my job.

The newspaper article appeared ten months after Carl came out to his friends and classmates. During that entire time his dad and I remained in the closet at work. That morning my boss came into my office and sat down. "Tell Carl congratulations on the scholarship."

"I wanted to tell you, but I couldn't." I still couldn't actually say, "Carl is gay," but my boss knew what I meant.

"Ruby, we are who we are."

A couple of minutes later another faculty member popped his head through the doorway. He asked me to congratulate Carl for him.

One of the few regrets I have about my coming out process is that I wish I had told my boss myself. He was my good friend, and I should have told him in person long before the article was published. No one threw eggs at our house. Paul didn't get beat up. I didn't lose my job. One of Carl's junior high teachers took him out to lunch to celebrate, another teacher sent a lovely congratulatory card and letter. Everyone was happy for him.

It's easy for family members to be in the closet. I was afraid of what people would or wouldn't say, what they would think about my child and my family. I was afraid of repercussions. I wasn't prepared to face the potential unpleasantness that could come my way. I worried I would hear hateful and judgmental remarks. Above this, though, I feared for both of my children's safety. I also worried that people would avoid me and the subject that I had a gay son. I was worried about everything — it's my nature to maximize worrying opportunities.

In the same way that I was greeted at work because of the *Journal* article, Leonard was congratulated by one of his colleagues. He had seen the article in the paper and asked Leonard to give Carl his congratulations. It was exactly what one would expect to have happen when coming into the office the morning an article about your child's achievements appears in the paper.

Sadly, though, only those three people at our work congratulated us. But it's not like we worked in any ordinary office setting. We both worked at the University of Alberta. Articles about students winning scholarships were of particular interest to many of our colleagues. But in 2004 there was still uneasiness about public declarations regarding homosexuality, even at the U of A. That was about to change.

Within a year Canadians were no longer able to avoid discussions about sexual orientation. Same-sex marriage legislation was tabled in the House of Commons; the subsequent vote would be scrutinized and debated from coast to coast. Intense opposition to the legislation was being orchestrated by fear-mongering fundamentalist religious, ethnic, and political groups as well as individuals who felt threatened by this change that would guarantee equal rights for all Canadians. Until the public debate was in full swing, Leonard and I cautiously waited for the right time to tell our friends and neighbours that our son was gay.

I wish I had told two other close friends, as well as my boss. Instead of hearing the news from me, my friends heard it from their kids. At a gathering of our families I sheepishly told my friends that Carl was gay and that I had wanted to tell them earlier but couldn't.

One of my friends replied that she understood. Her brother was gay.

Just as my son had worried about people's reactions, I was apprehensive too. Throughout my life, I've picked my friends carefully. I had no reason to believe they were homophobic, but I was still unsure about how they would react. When I told my friend I wanted to write about her comment that day, she said she would have to check with her brother to get his permission for the reference. Her first instinct was to protect her brother. My generation has a deeply rooted caution associated with homosexuality. This results from what we might have heard at home when we were growing up and definitely from what all of us saw and heard in our high school hallways. I couldn't stand it when my gay high school friends were harassed and yet I have no recollection of myself, or anyone else for that matter, standing up for our friends by telling the bullies to stop. Having a gay son helped me to begin digging myself out of decades of suffocating silence.

It became clear to me very quickly that everyone had an LGBT family member or friend and that most of us were in some way closeted, especially when a family member was involved. Some members of the LGBT community bristle when they hear reference to family members being in the closet. I don't know any better words or phrase to use to describe what it's like for us as parents or siblings. Although our situation is not the same as our child's, we too have to choose whether or not to disclose we have a gay child, and we have to decide when and how to do it, and then we hope for the best. In too many instances there is hurtful and negative fallout. Sexuality is generally a private matter. Up until same-sex marriage legislation was passed, homosexuality in Canada was treated as shameful. Until 1969 it was illegal. For many religions it is still considered a sin and is unacceptable. Today, as our children come out, we as families have to come out as well. Far too many children are still forced to hide, to protect their identity for fear of discrimination and we, the parents and families, are also forced to construct scenarios to help protect them. It is my hope that soon we will all be able to say, "She has a partner," instead of the euphemism, "She has a roommate."

III

FINDING OUR WAY

ON A SATURDAY EVENING IN JANUARY 2003, WITH A TERRIBLE BLIZZARD outside, when Carl had yet to come out to Paul, Leonard and I went to see a screening of the documentary *Standing in the Shadows of Motown*. The movie was about the Funk Brothers, the studio musicians, who provided the backup music for most of the great hit songs on Motown Records. We headed home with Motown tunes playing in our heads. When we got home, Paul, who had just turned fourteen, was in a panic. Before we could get our boots off and hang up our coats he told us that right after we left, Carl told him he was going downtown to a Second Cup on 106th Street to have coffee with somebody. Carl hadn't told the truth. There was no Second Cup on 106th Street. Paul had looked on the Internet and couldn't find it. Our kids didn't tattle on each other. Paul wasn't telling us this to get Carl in trouble. Paul knew something was wrong and was genuinely worried.

Normally, Carl would have said something like, "I want to meet Eric or Lisa or Michael for coffee tonight. Can I take the car and go to the Second Cup on Whyte Avenue at 7:00? I'll be home by 9:30." Leaving the house minutes after we left and making up a story about where he was going was not normal for him.

Paul imagined the only reason Carl could be going downtown and lying about it was to buy drugs. There wasn't any reason to suspect Carl had anything to do with drugs, but that was Paul's understanding of what people did in downtown Edmonton on Saturday night. He didn't consider any other possibility.

This was a time before every teenager in North America had a cellphone; we had no way of contacting Carl and had to wait anxiously for him to come home. To my relief he came through the door a few minutes later. Leonard and I decided we'd separate the boys. He would stay downstairs with Paul and I'd go upstairs with Carl to find out what was going on. Carl sat in the rocking chair in our bedroom and I sat cross-legged on the bed. I tried not to sound annoyed when I told him that his brother was really upset about him leaving the house. And then I asked him where he'd gone.

Carl was forthright. He had found an ad in *SEE Magazine* — the same magazine where I saw what I thought was a parent group ad — about a drop-in for teenagers at the gay and lesbian centre. He went there so he could talk to someone who knew what it felt like to be gay. He couldn't tell Paul where he was going so he said he was going downtown to meet a friend for coffee.

My first reaction was stunned silence, followed by heartbreak, and then disbelief. We had raised our children to know they were never to answer personal classified ads in newspapers.

After Leonard and I left, Carl got in the car and drove downtown to 106th Street and found the centre. It was in the back of an old office building, on the second floor. He had to walk down a long hallway at the end of which was a closed door. He wasn't sure if he was in the right place.

He opened the door and went in. There was only one kid. A few more came later. And two adults — a man and a woman who, it turned out, were the coordinators.

In total four kids were there. They sat in a circle and talked. He told them his name and that he attended Strathcona High School.

I was having trouble believing what I was hearing and tried desperately to stay calm. Carl had told these strangers his real name and what high school he attended.

I told him that he was naive to think this information would be safe. Had he thought about the possibility that the other kids might have friends at Scona? That they might call them and tell them they met him at a gay and lesbian centre?

Carl stayed calm and tried to explain. He needed to be with other people who were like him. He didn't know what would happen if these other kids did call their friends at Scona. But he couldn't think that was going to happen. Everyone there had said they felt like they have to hide all the time.

In spite of Carl's explanation, I was sure the kids who were at the group that night would be calling their friends at Strathcona to tell them they had met Carl and that he was gay. His dad and I were horrified he had searched for help in the classified ads of a tabloid, albeit an arts and entertainment tabloid. We were shaken by the fact that he had driven to a downtown address, without being certain of where he was going, and that he had walked into a place alleging to be for gay young people. I thought my heart was going to break. Carl was desperate to talk to someone who shared his reality and I had no idea how to help. Despite this realization, I repeatedly told him he should not have gone to the centre.

I had it all wrong. Looking back at my behaviour that night I realize I was irrational; but this was very early on. As a family, we were still in the closet and I was terrified for his safety. Carl didn't return to the centre until months later.

That winter, Carl was on a French-language exchange in Quebec for three months. For years provincial governments and school boards had promoted various language exchanges between French-speaking high school students in Quebec and the nine other English-speaking provinces in Canada. In September 2002, Andre from Havre-Saint-Pierre, Quebec came to live with us for three months while he attended Strathcona High School with Carl.

In February 2003, Carl flew from Edmonton to Montreal, over to Quebec City, and on to Sept-Iles where he was met by Andre and his parents. They then drove east for another two and a half hours along the north shore of the St. Lawrence River to Havre St. Pierre. This is a remote area — he was closer to Ireland than he was to Edmonton. After a good night's sleep Carl and Andre went to the rink for the day to watch three hockey games. The kids' priority that day was to teach Carl

French swear words while he ate platefuls of authentic poutine and five hot dogs.

Thirty-four hundred people lived in Havre St. Pierre. There was no English TV, radio, or newspaper service. The town had mail delivered twice a week. The snow was so deep, road crews regularly shoveled away blindingly white snow from the tops of STOP signs so they could be seen. It was a true French-immersion experience along with an introduction to living in a small town where, to my chagrin, he went snowmobiling in the dark, a popular and dangerous Canadian winter pastime.

Carl was becoming a fluent French speaker by living in rural Quebec. He toured Quebec City, Sept Iles, and small communities on the north shore of the St. Lawrence River with his host family. Meanwhile, his dad and I were becoming acquainted with gay issues and community resources back in Edmonton. We secretly attended PFLAG meetings. Through PFLAG we learned Youth Understanding Youth (YUY), the drop-in Carl had gone to, was legitimate, well run, and a good place for four-teen- to twenty-four-year-olds. I decided to investigate YUY. I had to lie to Paul about where I was going. I arrived shortly after seven p.m. and saw about twenty kids wearing jeans, T-shirts, hoodies, and sneakers. A couple had piercings, and one or two had fluorescent hair. There was one male and one female facilitator to supervise and coordinate the programming for the evening. Kris Wells, the male facilitator, who I later learned organized the group, greeted me. I explained I had a seventeen-year-old son who had attended a couple of months earlier and that I wanted to know about the program. Kris remembered Carl from January and spent half an hour telling me about himself, the other facilitators, and the purpose and philosophy of YUY. The conversation confirmed what we had been told at PFLAG, appeased my worries, and put my mind at ease.

Each YUY meeting had at least one male and one female facilitator present. They were typically teachers, nurses, social workers, counselors, and students. All were volunteers and had security clearances, as was generally the requirement when working with underage minors. The facilitators were trained to deal with kids in need and they also knew how to have fun.

YUY became an essential weekly part of Carl's life throughout grade twelve. There were weeks when sixty kids packed into a small gathering room. They all loved going and couldn't wait until the next week. Years later Carl told me all the kids had a crush on Kris, a good-looking, hip, cool thirty-one-year-old. Kris had the same effect on the YUY kids as the young creative, charismatic, popular teachers we all knew in high school. He was compassionate and passionate, had a clear vision about what he wanted to achieve, and was devoted to making the world a better place for LGBT youth.

A few years earlier, when Kris was a young teacher, an invisible gay student in his class took his own life. "When I was in high school I was invisible too," Kris said the night I scouted YUY. "No one knew I was gay. It was the same when I first started teaching. Neither the students nor the other teachers knew I was gay. My student's suicide drove me to find ways to assist sexual and gender minority students who have no adults to turn to for help." He went on to get his Ph.D. in Education at U of A in Educational Policy Studies. His research focused on sex, sexuality, and gender differences in kindergarten through grade twelve. His supervisor was Dr. Andre Grace, whose research had focused on the issues of inclusion and accommodation of sexual and gender minority students and teachers in education and culture. Together they were the cofounders and co-directors of Camp fYrefly (fostering, Youth, resiliency, energy, fun, leadership, yeah!) and the U of A's Institute for Sexual Minorities Studies and Services (isMSS), among numerous other initiatives.

Kris's career has centred on bringing awareness to issues of equality, acceptance and support for LGBT youth in the school system and beyond. He's made the world a better place for countless people and has likely saved lives. By helping one individual at a time he's worked to change human rights legislation, school board policies, and codes of conduct for teachers across Canada. I hope one day he will receive the Order of Canada.

Back when Carl was attending YUY, each evening started with circle time, where everyone got to share one positive thing and one negative thing from the previous week. For many kids this was the only opportunity to unload a problem or difficulty and get support from friends and the adult facilitators. Having to share something positive also helped the kids realize there were bright spots in their week. They had games nights, movie nights, pizza, guest speakers, barbeques, and camping and hiking trips. It was the best thing for Carl. Nothing could keep him away from YUY, where he made many great new friends, one or two of whom turned into boyfriends. Together with Kris's leadership, Carl and a few others went on to develop Camp fYrefly, a hugely successful four-day annual summer leadership retreat for LGBT youth that runs in Edmonton and Calgary and rotates between Saskatoon and Regina. After YUY the older kids went out for coffee, followed by dancing at the Roost, a gay dance club, which has since closed.

I can't imagine how desperate Carl must have felt that night in January when he left Paul at home, drove downtown, and walked down a long, dark corridor to meet a room full of strangers hoping to find someone he could relate to without having to explain anything. He found a community — one his heterosexual family could not provide.

Part Three

I

BOB AND JOHNNIE

EVERY YEAR, SENIOR UNIVERSITY ADMINISTRATORS FROM ACROSS CANADA gather at the Banff Centre in Banff National Park for a week-long academic administrators course, which I attended in the spring of 2004. At lunch on the first day I sat with Bob, one of the attendees, who mentioned the work of Richard Florida. Florida was a professor at the University of Toronto who devised a creative class-ranking system that suggested cities with concentrations of gays and lesbians, artists, and musicians as well as technology experts and foreign-born residents have higher economic development. Bob clearly supported Florida's theory and his ranking of a city's "gay index." When Bob and I were at the dessert table I whispered, "My son is gay." Bob, remaining intensely focused on a making a dessert decision, said, "Enhh, so am I."

As the days went by we learned Bob had been a professional opera singer, so all week long people pestered him to sing. At the wrap-up dinner he relented and sang an aria from an obscure Canadian LGBT comic opera, *The Loves of Wayne Gretzky*. The opera portrays two great Canadian hockey icons, Wayne Gretzky and Mario Lemieux, in a gay relationship where Wayne leaves his wife, Janet, for Mario. I was at Bob's table that evening. The combination of his beautiful tenor voice and his graphic interpretation of the lyrics, with a particularly creative investigation of hockey sticks, got everyone's attention. As Bob took his seat beside me there was a delay of a few seconds before anyone laughed or clapped. No one requested an encore.

The next morning at breakfast, a course participant asked the rest of us at the table if we thought we would get complaints if Bob performed that song at a staff event at one of our institutions. Several people commented, focusing less on the performance the night before and how it would go over at their institutions, and more on their own opinions about Bob's sexuality.

In response one of them muttered, "What was his rationale for selecting a gay song?"

Another added, "His depiction was graphic. The lyrics had gay sexual connotations. What was his intention?"

What they really meant was, "He proved it last night. He's gay." Camouflaged as discussing whether or not straight people are too sensitive to witness a performance of a gay opera, what they were actually saying was, "Bob's a fag."

They didn't stop. No one came to Bob's defence to speculate that Bob could have picked that aria because he wanted to have fun or that it might have been something he had recently performed and knew. No one, including me, defended his choice by pointing out that nearly every opera revolves around love or sex. The exchange was like a scene from the movie *Mean Girls*, except the conversation participants were highly educated men and women instead of high school girls.

I sat there transfixed while the room began to spin around me. Voices seemed muffled and at the same time it sounded as if they were being amplified through an echo chamber. I couldn't think, and I couldn't speak. In a daze, I picked up my tray and left the table.

An hour later on the airport shuttle I told my friend Melanie, another course participant, about the breakfast conversation. "Those fucking homophobes," said Melanie while looking straight ahead.

I started to cry. I tried everything in my power to stop crying. I cried all the way to the airport, at the desk and departure gate, during the flight home, in the car on the way home, and all evening at home. When I woke up the next day, I cried all day. It took me a day and a half to stop crying. For the preceding eighteen months I had been consumed with the fear Carl would be bullied at school, that kids would be whispering about him behind his back. That day, right in front of me, university-educated people talked about their colleague's sexuality in an uncharitable, judgmental way. This was early on in our family's coming-out process, when only a few days earlier I had mustered the courage to whisper to Bob that my son was gay. I didn't yet have the experience or confidence to tell them to stop pretending they were talking about workplace conduct when they were actually discussing Bob's sexuality. He was gay and it made them uncomfortable. Surrounded by individuals I assumed would lead the way for equality, I instead experienced a profound sense of betrayal.

I was disappointed and heartbroken that senior university educators and administrators, who saw themselves as forward-thinking academic leaders, were nothing more than homophobes with good vocabularies. They seemed to feel they could justify their comments by couching the exchange in academic language. This was the academic variant of, "I call it the way I see it" or, "I'm just saying what everyone is thinking." Would they have made those cruel remarks if Bob had been sitting at the breakfast table with them? Does "academic freedom" mean you are entitled to talk about people behind their backs? Bearing witness to the conversation was profoundly discouraging.

Years later I relayed the conversation to Bob and his partner, Johnnie, to ask their permission to write about what had happened. I avoided the call for months, as I was worried hearing about the comments would hurt Bob's feelings. When I called, Bob and Johnnie listened to my recollections of the aria and we laughed. Next I had to tell them about the breakfast conversation and my reaction. "They never would have made the comments if Bob had been there," I told them. Johnnie responded that that's what homophobia is like: the comments are never made when the gay person is there.

To Bob and Johnnie, men in their fifties and sixties, this behaviour was typical. They had endured such treatment their entire lives and weren't surprised by what I revealed.

"The irony here is half the men on campus are gay," Bob said. "I think at least one of the men at the table that morning was gay."

Johnnie told me that there had been a big change since 2003. He wanted me to believe this wouldn't be something Carl would have to learn to live with.

When I told Leonard about Bob and Johnnie's reaction to the breakfast conversation and how they saw it as commonplace and predictable behaviour, both our eyes filled with tears. To cope, the men had become desensitized to verbal abuse. The people at the breakfast table had made cruel comments and behaved shamefully. Ignorance knows no socioeconomic boundaries.

Bob and Johnnie had been together for over thirty years. They jokingly said they had waited twenty-five years to get married to make sure it was right. In reality, they got married two months after the Canadian Parliament passed Bill C-38, which provided a gender-neutral definition of marriage, legalizing same-sex marriage across the nation. When I asked them how it felt to be married, Johnnie told me the commitment and love were always there, but after years of hiding, having equal standing in society — having the same rights and the same social acceptance as everyone else — was profound to him.

With a laugh Bob said, "I did it to keep Johnnie happy." Adding, "I like putting on my wedding ring in the morning. But, I panic when I realize I've left it at the gym."

Bob's family and mine became close friends. The summer Carl and I attended Carl's University of Toronto new student orientation, Bob, Johnnie, Carl, and I went out for dinner on Queen Street West followed by a walking tour of Queen Street heading east. We were tired of walking and took a short cab ride to Church Street, the gay village area in Toronto. In the cab, Johnnie, who has a playful sense of humour, decided instead of saying "gay" when the word came up in the conversation we should say "dolphin." As in, "We're heading to the Toronto dolphin area."

I wondered, "Are the streets going to be filled with dolphins tonight?"

Between howls of laughter, Carl pondered, "Are there many dolphin bars and restaurants?"

"I'd like to see the Dolphin Pride Centre," I added. The cab driver paid no attention to us and manoeuvred through traffic.

It was a beautiful July evening and the streets were packed with people. We walked past the 519 Church Street Community Centre, Toronto's gay and lesbian centre. Johnnie guided us into Cawthra Square Park, a little park beside the community centre and away from the crowds. (The park has since been renamed Barbara Hall Park.) We quietly strolled through the park's Toronto AIDS Memorial — a series of triangular columns with the names of loved ones lost to HIV/AIDS inscribed on plaques. A few names were listed under each year in the early eighties. By the end of the decade, hundreds and hundreds of names appeared under each year. The names are sorted by the year of death only and are not alphabetized, encouraging visitors to read thousands of names on the columns. With the concern of a father and love in his voice, Johnnie softly said to Carl that he and Bob had lost many friends to AIDS. He told him to make sure this didn't happen to him.

Carl was invited to their wedding ceremony in 2005 along with many other friends and relatives. Johnnie's cousin's daughter Emelene, who was six years old, attended the ceremony with her parents. Soon after, two boys in Emelene's grade one class, who were best friends, announced they were getting married. Kids in the class told them they couldn't get married because they were both boys. Emelene corrected her classmates: "Yes, two boys can get married. My dad's cousin is a man and he married a man." Emelene had proof.

My Son Is Gay

KISSING IN THE MARSHALING AREA ⌐

I WAS CURIOUS TO KNOW WHEN CARL FIRST THOUGHT OR FELT HE KNEW HE was gay. He told me he knew he was different from the other kids in his class when he was in grade six, about eleven or twelve years old, and that he knew he was gay at the end of the summer between grades 10 and 11.

As he was growing up he always had boys, and a few girls, as friends. When he was five he wanted to marry his friend Caroline. "She's always nice to me," he'd say. In junior high he liked a couple of girls. In high school he said of his close childhood friend Meghan, who lived on our street, "She's perfect. Everyone would like to date her." But he never dated or asked any of the girls out. Years later Carl would be the MC at Meghan's wedding and she would name him the godfather of her baby girl.

Carl had a couple other early memories. When he was four years old he looked furtively at a bare chested Jim Morrison on a Doors album cover in the jukebox at Earl's Restaurant, where our family were regular patrons. He also remembered that he liked driving home from downtown on River Valley Road because there was a good chance we'd see bare-chested men running or bike riding on the trails. At the time I thought he preferred what I called "the scenic route" because of the trees and golf course in our beautiful, massive, river valley.

For weeks each spring, in preparation for the Pride Parade, the YUY kids made dozens of rainbow-coloured buttons, bracelets, and pins to give away to people who came out to watch the parade. Carl, along with the YUY kids and adult facilitators, marched in the 2004 Edmonton Pride Week Parade. They had a banner and bags full of loot to give away. Until that day, no one in our family had watched, never mind marched in, the parade. A year earlier, in 2003, we were still in the closet and before that it had never occurred to us to go out and show our support for the LGBT community. I was a little worried about him participating in the parade but told myself he was there with a group, and Kris and several other facilitators were supervising the activities. I did my best to convince myself nothing ugly would happen to them along the parade route with religious extremists, protestors, or run-of-the-mill homo-phobes, who at that time were always highly visible with their religious slogans on placards and derogatory protest signs.

It was a perfect June day in Edmonton. The kids and Kris were gath-ered in a parking lot a couple of blocks north of the Alberta Legislature Building, which sits regally on the expansive steep banks of the North Saskatchewan River. Especially before noon in this part of Canada, we usually have crystal clear blue skies with a lazy cloud here and there slowly drifting by. Parade day was no exception; it was a perfect twenty degrees. The giant old elms lining the boulevards were flush with vibrant green leaves. The tree limbs embraced the excited kids, forming a perfect portrait of summer as the YUYers scurried around preparing for the parade.

I dropped Carl off in the parade marshaling area around noon. Every-one welcomed him with hugs, then returned to decorating each other with rainbow face paints and tattoos, and the YUY banner with rainbow streamers and balloons.

As I drove away I could see Carl and his boyfriend in my rearview mirror. He was kissing the person he was dating — another young man. This wasn't a peck on the cheek. The two of them were in each other's arms engaged in a long display of affection. When I was in high school, in rural Saskatchewan, what they were doing would have been described as necking. The image of Carl and his boyfriend kissing that day is forever burned in my memory. It was the single event that convinced me my son was in fact gay. I don't think accepting I had a gay child was the issue for me. Rather, fundamentally I didn't believe he was gay and was actually hoping he just thought he was gay. But you couldn't kiss someone like that unless it felt right. This wasn't a phase. It wasn't something he was trying out. At that moment, I knew for certain my son was gay.

The event made me afraid and sad. Only a month earlier my professional world had collapsed around me when I witnessed sophisticated homophobia at the university administrators course in Banff. On parade morning I worried the kids would be the targets of harassment and violence along the route. Carl's open display of affection, a natural human behaviour, could actually lead to a beating. He could be affectionate in the marshaling area but I didn't know if he would ever be able to walk down the street holding hands with another man without worrying about being harassed. Why is it okay for me to walk down the street holding hands with my husband but not okay for Carl and his partner? How and when did a natural display of affection become a threat or prohibited? I felt like I was being suffocated by bigotry and wondered how my dear, sweet boy would survive in an often-cruel world. I kept driving and cried all the way home.

Our experiences with Carl and his boyfriends have been no different than our experiences with Paul and his girlfriends. During high school, Carl and a boyfriend regularly watched TV downstairs and cuddled — they were cute, it was nice. I wasn't particularly fond of the boy he was dating at the end of grade twelve because he was a fourth-year university student. Why was a university student dating a high school student? The age difference was too wide for me to feel comfortable. We had met a few of his boyfriends during our early visits to Toronto. One of them invited me over to see the apartment he was sharing with three other roommates. No surprises there, either. Dishes, clothes, shoes, books, and laptops were strewn everywhere, familiar housekeeping practices in all student-housing situations. When my sons are happy, I'm happy. When my sons have relationship problems, I ache along with them. He dated young men I liked and others that made me think, I'm glad that's over. Like mothers sometimes do, over the years I also suggested and even introduced him to young men I thought he might like to get to know — this strategy rarely works.

III

Ask but Don't Tell

IN GENERAL CARL HAS BEEN OPEN ABOUT HIS SEXUALITY. HE STARTED THE GSA, declared he was gay friendly/positive on his university residence application, and joined University of Toronto LGBT student clubs and sports teams. He was out at all jobs with the exception of one short part-time job he had on the furniture and equipment moving crew at U of T where he did not feel it was safe to disclose.

For us, Carl being out has also meant enduring the "I don't have a problem with gay people" comment. I've often felt like saying, "Gee, thanks," as the comment reminds me that until as recently as the 1970s many people thought it was okay to say, "I don't have a problem with women working outside the home." I know in some circles this notion is still commonplace. Both comments originate from people who've made the fundamental assumption that for a segment of the population it is acceptable to have a problem with gays or with women working outside the home. Then they think they're doing a favour by saying they're not part of that segment. Some people are sincerely trying to be nice and genuinely mean well, but far too often these statements are followed by comments like, "He can do whatever he wants with his life" — as if he had a choice.

Carl says he's looking forward to the day when his sexuality is not something he needs to disclose or discuss. I'm also eager for a time when Carl's sexuality is no longer seen as something distinct. It doesn't matter to me whether my children share their lives with men or women. They have the right to be happy by doing what feels right for them.

LESBIAN SISTER / GAY BROTHER ∽

During carl's last year in high school, one of my neighbours and I were standing in her entrance and got talking about teaching kids how to vacuum and clean bathrooms. She said my sons' wives are going to be happy they know how to clean bathrooms.

This was a perfect opportunity for me to let her know things were different at our house. I told her it wouldn't be just wives.

"Actually, the kids told me," she replied. "It's fine with our family." By pretending she didn't know, she gave me the opportunity to choose whether or not I wanted to disclose Carl's sexuality. She then asked how I felt about having a gay son.

I thought we were laughing about reminding kids to use rubber gloves when cleaning the bathroom. Suddenly I was being asked how I felt about my son's sexuality. At that stage in our family's coming-out process this wasn't a topic I was prepared to talk about with someone who did not have an LGBT child. I wasn't going to avoid the question, but I wanted to end the discussion. "This is the way it is." I had nothing else to say and thankfully she let it go.

A couple of years after Carl came out Leonard and I became open to discussions about LGBT issues, but I would still need to learn that if the timing, relationship, or circumstances weren't right, I wasn't required to talk about anything I didn't want to talk about. I figured out a few exit strategies to easily end a conversation or leave the discussion. Simple excuses about having to get back to work, or make a phone call, or get to the dessert table before all the chocolate is gone work great. I got away if the conversation didn't feel right. At the start it was most helpful for Leonard and me to talk about how we felt when we were with PFLAG parents. Looking back at the discussion with my neighbour, even if this were an appropriate question for her to have asked, she couldn't have comprehended the answer had I been able to articulate a response. You can't completely understand how it feels to have a gay child until you experience it yourself.

About a year later, the same neighbour's sister's marriage ended. The sister had left her husband and son and come out as lesbian. To show their support, another family member invited the lesbian sister, Carl, and some high-school-aged nieces and nephews over to watch a few episodes of *Will and Grace*, a TV sitcom featuring Will, a young gay professional. Carl, then in first-year university, had not previously met the lesbian sister, who was old enough to be his mother.

When Carl came home he told me they watched TV, but he had nothing else to say. Two LGBT people in a room together are not necessarily going relate to each other or bond. I've since had conversations with the same family about their sister's new job and where she's living. There has never been a right time to ask how she feels about having a lesbian sister. Quite honestly, though, I actually don't want to ask the question. Discussing someone's sibling's or child's sexuality is not a casual conversation topic. To disclose that I had an LGBT family member was a personal and private decision. As much as possible Leonard and I have picked the times, the amount of information, and the people with whom we shared our family circumstances.

As time passed, everyone at work learned I had become involved with PFLAG. In addition to periodically responding to telephone calls from counselors and teachers, I often did TV and newspaper interviews or left work to participate in panel discussions. Staff members, colleagues, and neighbours began to see me as a safe person with whom they could share their own stories or concerns about LGBT family members.

Bit by bit over a period of two and half years a staff member, who was my age, disclosed she had a gay brother. Occasionally she'd come into my office to privately confess another detail about him. Eventually she told me he had died when he was in his mid-thirties. Because she hadn't known anyone who was gay, she never suspected her unmarried brother was gay. He only told the family he was gay when he was dying. It tortured her to admit he had died in the mid-eighties as a result of HIV/AIDS. I'm sure I was the only one at work who knew about her deeply private family sorrow and the shame she felt. She never told me his name.

WHAT BAD MEANS IN THE SWANSON HOUSE ～

"I had bad luck" was how my dad explained cutting three fingers off his left hand. When the crops failed my parents always said, "Next year we'll get something." Sometimes the crops were better, sometimes not.

"There's nothing better for me than to watch the sun set on my land," my dad told my mother-in-law the first time he met her. "In the evening everything will be quiet except for a couple of birds talking to each other across the hills." He smiled as he sat on the Swanson's piano bench describing the life and land he loved. Drawing a broad, sweeping line with his outstretched right arm and a hand with all five fingers, he told her that the whole horizon is orange in the fall. My mother-in-law thought he was a poet.

In the fall of 1983 my dad went to the farm, just like he had every morning of his life. He loved the farm and had a bumper crop that year. Harvest was over early and it was time to haul bales in late September. Hauling bales was easy since he'd purchased an automatic bale loader. The loader scooped up small rectangular bales that were fed along a conveyor and lined up neatly on a flatbed. When the flatbed was full the bed automatically swung ninety degrees, placing the bales in tidy rows on a large rack. When the rack was full, he'd drive over to the main stack to unload. The bales had to fit perfectly in place to keep the stack from falling over.

After lunch my aunt, who lived on the farm next to ours, saw Dad moving equipment from our home quarter section of land to another quarter three kilometres south. It was hot that day, nearly twenty-six degrees Celsius, when Dad, comfortable inside the cab of his air-conditioned tractor, glanced over his shoulder and saw a bale out of line on the top row of the rack. Always in a hurry and never bothering with safety, he went straight to the rack instead of putting the safety latch on to keep the hydraulic from engaging. The hydraulic bed, engaged, came back down, struck his head, and pinned him to the frame of the loader, where he died instantly. Minutes later, a farmer Dad had spoken with that morning came driving onto the field. The frantic man dislodged the loader's flatbed, but it was too late. He jumped back into his truck and drove to the nearest farm and called the police. The RCMP delivered the terrible news to my mom and sister at my sister's business. Crying uncontrollably, my sister called me at work. "I have terrible news. Daddy's dead." My dad had become another farm fatality statistic.

My coworker immediately booked a flight home for Leonard and me. She and her husband gave us a ride to the airport. Less than five hours after my sister had called, Leonard and I were at Mom's side. One of the most important people in my mother's life had been taken away from her with no warning. Leonard and I walked into her darkened bedroom where she sat alone on the edge of her bed. "What am I going to do without him?" she said, looking up at me in disbelief.

That night I lay in bed thinking this is what it must be like to live in a war zone where the inconceivable happens every day. I was in shock for two solid months. I couldn't remember if I had eaten, opened the mail, heard from my family, or picked up a carton of milk. I don't know how I functioned at work. For years after his death I automatically hoped my dad was calling when the phone rang and looked through the back door to see if his truck was in the driveway whenever we were at my parents' house.

My sons never met my father but they have a sense of the kind of man he was and the kind of father he was to me. Dad died two days after my twenty-ninth birthday. Leonard only knew him for four years. I have several photos of Dad in our den. My favourite shot is of him sleeping on the back steps the day we moved into the first house Leonard and I bought. Dad could fall asleep anywhere within two minutes. He sat in the shade with his back against the prickly crushed stone and cut glass stucco wall and fell sound asleep with his arms crossed over his chest, one leg dangling and the other leg bent at the knee with his foot anchored to keep him from sliding off the landing. I won a photo of the month contest with that image. I've told my sons countless stories about my dad, many good and some not so good.

My dad was eccentric and a Dr. Doolittle of sorts. A small herd of sheep roamed freely in our farmyard so he wouldn't have to cut the grass. "I wanted to try out my new wool shears" was his explanation for shearing Tina, our copper-coloured Pekingese dog. She looked like a box of Kleenex when he was done. He kept exotic guinea hens and bantam roosters because they looked nice and he trained the cattle to come to him when he honked the horn on his truck.

Our farmyard was huge. My parents built a two-bedroom, cottage style, wood-frame house in 1954 complete with a white picket fence. The house sat at the top of a hill facing east with the morning sun streaming in through the kitchen window above the sink. At the bottom of the hill was a small slough with a little bluff of trees on the north edge of the water. Year round my brother and I played in the trees. In winter Dad cleared off the slough for us to skate. The hill on the north side of the slough was great for tobogganing. When we came in from tobogganing, Mom sat us on chairs in front of the open oven door of our wood burning stove where we warmed up sipping cups of hot Nestlé's Quik.

The night before Dad's funeral we made a care package of his favourite stuff for him to have at his side in his casket. Every kid in town knew he always had Doublemint gum in the front pocket of his blue jeans or overalls, so we made sure he had a fresh pack. We included hard candies and jujubes, a favourite cap, a handful of toothpicks, and a phone book — he used to spend hours sitting at the kitchen table, beside our orange rotary dial wall phone, calling people. He'd call me in the middle of the day at work to say hi. If he were alive today he'd have the best cellphone on the market.

Had he been more careful, Dad wouldn't have died that day at the farm. The accident wouldn't have happened had the farmer who found him arrived fifteen minutes earlier. Had my brother-in-law gone out to the farm with him that day ...

None of this will bring him back. Even though he's gone, even though my boys never met him, they know they would have had lots of fun with their grandfather. They also know everything I know about what happened at the farm that afternoon.

MY FAMILY DOCTOR TOOK care of me through both my pregnancies and up until her retirement in 2015. We knew each other for over thirty years and saw each other at least once a year for my annual physical examination. "How is Leonard's health?" was one of her routine questions.

Leonard was thirty-three years old in 1990 when he was diagnosed with stage 4B non-Hodgkin's lymphoma. That was the highest and worst classification — 4B. It meant he had a tumor larger than ten centimetres and there were cancer cells throughout his body, including in his bone marrow. He had surgery to remove the tumor and developed pneumonia. Two days after he was discharged his lung collapsed. Carl was four years old and Paul was thirteen months old.

The oncologists recommended immediate chemotherapy as Leonard had an aggressive form of cancer that responded well to treatment.

My dad had died unexpectedly and now I thought Leonard was going to die too. To make matters worse, Leonard needed a blood transfusion during the tainted blood scandal in Canada. I added contracting HIV/AIDS to the list of things that could kill one or both of us and leave our children orphaned. I hoped Leonard's medical team could keep him alive for a couple more years so I would have time to create a few memories of their dad for Carl and Paul. We did everything together as a family.

Leonard recovered and went back to work full time. Not long afterwards I got a part-time job working three evenings a week. Leonard had the chance to be on his own with the boys in the evening and could take care of them in ways that worked for him. He had always been responsible for evening baths and reading to the boys at bedtime. The three of them developed their own menu for bedtime snacks. Why settle for a slice of fruit when you could have a bowl of ice cream or nachos with layers and layers of melted cheese?

Leonard felt good, my fear diminished, and then in the spring of 1996 he developed a cough. After two months of persistent coughing his doctor ordered an ultrasound. He was diagnosed with Hodgkin's disease, a different lymphoma with more tumors that required more chemo. "It's like being struck by lightning twice in one lifetime," his oncologist explained. This time the boys were seven and ten years old, old enough to know what was going on. Me saying, "Daddy's going to be sick for a long time before he gets better," didn't put their minds at ease. Every kid in the world is afraid his or her parents are going to die. The Swanson boys had a good reason to worry. I was sure Leonard was going to die this time. I consciously thought about a funeral and where he would be buried. Carl had nightmares for a few weeks before I made an appointment for the whole family to see a counselor at the Cancer Clinic.

"Do you think your dad is going to die?" the counselor asked the boys.

When both of them said "yes" I knew for certain that life was cruel and felt like I would never be able to stop crying. How could it be that my innocent children had a valid reason to believe their dad was going to die?

I went back into high gear, creating more memories of life with Daddy. I have thousands of photos of the boys with their dad. The boys always knew when Dad's checkups were coming up and we called with the results while we walked home. As long as Dad was alive things were good at our house.

Leonard's main side effect from receiving massive doses of chemotherapy was debilitating fatigue. He began to work part time so he had energy left for us when he got home at the end of the day. The next twelve years went by quickly without me having to act on my funeral plans. Then, in a six-week period in 2009, our dog died, Paul's twenty-two-year-old friend who had been diagnosed with cancer a few months earlier died, Leonard's dad died, and Leonard was diagnosed with a third cancer, marginal zone lymphoma. This one, we were told, occurs in people who have compromised immune systems. More chemo. Worst of all, the medical team told us from the start they wouldn't be able to get rid of it. Leonard was actually going to be living with cancer for the rest of his life.

During round three the boys turned twenty-one and twenty-four years old. I tried to get them to talk. The counselor told me the boys would try to protect me and would never open up about the fear of losing their dad. She was right. I couldn't get them to talk to me about how they felt, so every few weeks I wrote to them.

October 28, 2009

My dear boys,

This year we've had more than our share of sadness, disappointments, and worries. From the perspective of someone who has been on this earth more than twice as long as the two of you, I just want to say we will get through this very, very difficult time and things will be better. I'm not clairvoyant, I just know that throughout life there are rough patches and things always get better.

A few weeks ago I told Dad that I didn't mean to be greedy but I needed him to live for at least another twenty years. Yesterday he said me saying this was the best thing that could have happened because, he says, he always does what I tell him to do (I wish). In spite of all of the squabbling that you two have endured from us (me and Dad) I do have a way of giving approval or directing Dad with some of the bigger things in his life. When he had that terrible reaction to his first dose of Retuxamab, the nurses said he would be better in ten minutes. I kept track of every minute and could see at seven minutes just by looking at him that the Benadryl was working and things were under control. I said, "Leonard, you're okay now," and his whole body relaxed because he trusts me. He is very good about disciplining himself and accomplishing what for others, would not be "accomplishable."

So Carl, keep calling Dad, he loves your calls. Paul, Dad loves every minute he spends with you.

XOXOXO
Mom

Each time I sent the emails they'd call or write back instantly to tell me how great they felt reading what I had written to them.

We've had twenty-six years of cancer. I told everyone about it each time because I needed to surround myself with supportive people who didn't pity us. For years it was the first thing anyone asked about. Between the second and third bouts Leonard broke his leg skiing and hobbled around using a cane — everyone thought he had cancer. Since round three no one knows how to react when I say, "Leonard has cancer right now and it's not being treated. Watched yes, treated no." His overall health is either unbelievably good or unbelievably bad, depending on perspective. I'll go with good ... considering.

I talk about the complicated and difficult things. I confess to having a husband that has had/is living with cancer. I've tried to give my sons an idea and some understanding of their grandfather, including the tragic circumstances of his death. These are not secrets and it's no one's fault. Initially, I irrationally blamed my homesickness in New York for causing Leonard's illness. I thought if we had stayed in New York and not moved to western Canada, where there were high rates of lymphoma, he would have stayed healthy. There was no rational explanation for a thirty-three-year-old with advanced stage cancer. Avoiding hardship, pretending it's not there, didn't help me cope. I knew I had to prepare my boys, and myself, for the possibility of life without Dad and also I knew I had do it in a way that didn't scare them or damage them for the rest of their lives. Had the worst happened and Leonard died, I knew I would keep his memory alive forever.

During round two Leonard and I brought the boys to an appointment at the cancer clinic to meet their dad's doctor. He happened to be the father of Carl's classmate. We wanted them to see how the clinic looked inside to help remove the mystery of what happened when Dad went there every two weeks. They had been to the counseling area and cafeteria; it was okay to see the waiting, examination, and chemo rooms as well. Before Leonard had cancer simply driving by the cancer clinic made me shiver. I thought the people dropped off at the front door were going there to die. Overnight I became forever grateful the clinic was in our neighbourhood and I worshipped the healthcare professionals and researchers who dedicated their lives to the study of the disease.

Cancer was not a ghost in our house. We met it head on. It helped that Leonard kept on living. During Leonard's first bout of cancer Carl was only four years old. Carl knew his dad was going to be sick for a long time. In March that year he asked if Leonard was still going to be sick at Christmas. I told him he'd be better when we plant our garden; that was over two months away. I could have said, "Daddy is getting better every day" and tried to gloss things over. Daddy was only midway through chemotherapy and getting weaker every day — a four-year-old could see that.

Our sons would say that having cancer does not mean you are going to die. They've got proof.

Other questions my doctor routinely asked included, "How are things in general?" and, "Is there anything you want to mention that I need to write down?"

A few years after Carl came out I said, "Did I tell you Carl is gay?"

"Yes you did," she said, not looking up, still writing in my chart. "Are you over that yet?"

"Yeah ... I think so," I said, smiling, then laughing as I shook my head at her direct question. It was particularly satisfying for me that, although

I had no recollection of having mentioned it in the past, I clearly had and she remembered. She knew me well enough to sense it was taking me a little bit of time to figure things out and get comfortable.

I initially felt pressured to admit, sometimes I felt I had to confess, my son was gay. I did it to protect myself from hearing anyone say anything homophobic. I did it to advocate on my son's behalf. I did it to force the issue with people, thereby forcing them to get over it. I did it with my doctor because for her to properly care for me she had to know about life at our house. Just as I had told her about Leonard's bouts of cancer, I wanted my doctor to know my son was gay and had to laugh at myself for forgetting we had already had the conversation.

Part Four

I

Sixties Homophobia
and Eighties aids

PEARSON / TRUDEAU / TURNER ᕴ

When Carl was coming out I genuinely worried for his safety. Thirty years after graduating from high school, I was incapable of recognizing it was no longer the sixties and seventies and that society had moved beyond the fear of the aids epidemic during the eighties and nineties. My perception of LGBT issues had not evolved with the times and my mindset was stuck in the 1970 classrooms of my high school where I witnessed my friends endure harassment every day.

Homosexuality was illegal when I started high school in 1968. Gay males were referred to as homos and queers. The word queer was used with disgust and loathing. A year before, in 1967, Pierre Elliot Trudeau was the Minister of Justice in Prime Minister Lester B. Pearson's cabinet. In 1967 Trudeau introduced a bill that would make sweeping reforms to the Criminal Code of Canada. The reforms included decriminalizing homosexuality and abortion, loosening divorce laws, and over a hundred other amendments. During the countrywide debate Trudeau made his famous statement, "There is no place for the state in the bedrooms of the nation." The bill died as a result of an election call. After Trudeau was elected prime minister, Bill C-150, a 126-page omnibus document, was tabled in Parliament by Minister of Justice John Turner. Both Turner and Trudeau were Catholics. As a young man Turner had considered entering the priesthood. The abortion amendments were particularly difficult for Turner on a personal level. When he spoke to the bill he said that if law and order do not respond to change, yesterday's order becomes tomorrow's oppression. He recognized that the bill took a stand on controversial questions pertaining to our personal lives and issues of understanding, emphasizing that in a pluralist society everyone must strive to reconcile their own opinions and personal beliefs.

Bill C–150 passed with a clear majority of 149 to 55 on May 14, 1969, six weeks before the Stonewall riots in New York City.

In the 1990s the LGBT community had begun to use the word queer to identify and define themselves to provide a broader, more encompassing term that acknowledged the diversity beyond LGBT. For many people of my generation, queer was and remains an offensive word. In the early years after Carl came out, it made my skin crawl when I heard queer used by anyone. I've become a bit desensitized as a result of its rampant use within the community. In North America members of the LGBT community, such as my son, who uses the word routinely, tell me it's okay to say queer now. I am a Ukrainian-Canadian. My great grandparents came to this country in 1899. When I grew up in the 1960s Ukrainian-Canadians were still routinely referred to as dirty bohunks. Thankfully, my sons had never even heard the word bohunk and didn't have a clue what it meant until I brought it up. I don't know if there is a movement afoot to reclaim bohunk, but I hope not as I have never heard it used in a positive context. My experience with the usage of queer had been the same as my experience with the usage of bohunk. Therefore, I don't use queer to describe my son and the LGBT community.

GAY/AIDS/DEATH ↲

One of the main reasons people my age and older worry when they learn their child is gay is that in the early 1980s, when we were in our twenties, AIDS was an incurable epidemic that quickly killed thousands of gay men in North America. For the first twenty years during the epidemic, gay meant AIDS, which meant death. My mother's matter-of-fact statement, "It's all right that you are gay, but I don't want you to get AIDS and die," reflected the feeling people had. There was no effective treatment for decades. People suffered, wasted away, and died. There's still no cure, but several drugs are available to effectively treat many symptoms and researchers are working to develop a vaccine.

The general attitude among young people has shifted to the point where in 2013 a well-informed, healthy, twenty-eight-year-old straight man told me that today, AIDS is irrelevant. Not everyone agrees with this opinion. Protection is still the most effective way of preventing the spread of the human immunodeficiency virus (HIV) and acquired immuno-deficiency syndrome (AIDS) as well as other sexually transmitted infections. Healthcare professionals recommend anyone, gay or straight, who has had unprotected sex with multiple partners follow up regularly with their physician.

AIDS seemed to come out of nowhere, first being identified in the United States. The epidemic moved quickly from the gay community to intravenous drug users and then eventually to the general population in countries all over the world. African countries seem to be the least able to cope with the rapid spread of the disease. The AIDS hysteria lasted fifteen years, almost an entire generation. In the eighties and nineties members of fundamentalist religious groups and many politicians had a heyday with AIDS. To them, the disease was proof God was punishing gays for their sin of existence. Jerry Falwell, an American televangelist and cofounder of the Moral Majority, famously commented that AIDS is not God's punishment for homosexuals, it is God's punishment for the society that tolerates homosexuals. For decades, the hate he preached infected people all over the United States and Canada.

To make things worse, in the eighties the Canadian Red Cross blood donor service failed to properly test donated blood and blood products. They ignored indications there were serious problems with their processes, which resulted in further transmission of HIV as well as Hepatitis C to patients who had required blood transfusions and received tainted blood products.

Some were quick to think gay people caused the tainted blood scandal. In fact, it was caused by mismanagement on behalf of the people in charge of blood collection. In the summer of 1990, Leonard received a life-saving blood transfusion that was necessary to help him recover from the debilitating effects of the chemotherapy he had received to treat non-Hodgkin's lymphoma. He was terrified to think there was a possibility he could be receiving tainted blood that could give him HIV/AIDS, which he could in turn pass on to me. It was an uncertain time for people with serious health problems. Before his transfusion several health care professionals assured us there was no risk in receiving the blood. Yet, shortly after, more tainted blood scandals broke. Two years after his transfusion, Leonard received a letter in the mail telling him he was part of an at-risk group due to the transfusion and needed to be tested for Hepatitis C. We had another fear to live with: was there an HIV virus in his body that was not being detected? Not until 1992 was advanced testing put in place so the public could be assured blood and blood products were safe to use. Nonetheless, Leonard, for the next five years, worried the blood he received to save his life might end up killing him. Fortunately, he tested negative, but that did little to ease our concern at the time.

In the mid-nineties, the morning show on CBC Radio Edmonton aired a weekly testimonial by Michael, a man who had AIDS. At first I dreaded the segment — it was too sad and heartbreaking to hear a sick man, who we all knew was going to die, tell us about his symptoms, treatments, and how he coped. As the weeks and months went by I began to admire and eventually love him. As Michael grew weaker he began to miss tapings and then, to my relief he'd be back on the air. Then one morning the hosts told us the series was over because Michael had died. Tears silently streamed down my face as I went about getting the boys their breakfast and out the door for school. That series put a human name on the disease for me. Until then the only exposure I had had to AIDS was reports on radio and TV, and newspaper articles. The coverage recited the latest death tolls and featured interviews with emaciated men who begged and pleaded for more research into the disease, believing someone would discover something that would give them a glimmer of hope for survival following diagnosis. For the last two decades of the twentieth century, AIDS was a death sentence.

There are a couple of generations of people who automatically link "gay" with AIDS and death. As a result, gay males face blatant discrimination as blood donors. Before Carl came out he had donated blood once in high school. He was so proud to be able to do this because he knew how important it was for his dad to have blood available when he needed it. After he came out, while he was still in high school, he was no longer an eligible donor and was refused. The Canadian Blood Service, a group formed after the tainted blood scandal to take over blood collection from the Canadian Red Cross, made it clear they would not take his blood — by his sheer existence, his blood was under suspicion of being tainted. How damaging was this message to a young person? Being turned away as a donor devastated Carl and it infuriated and hurt me. It was the first incidence of open, legislated, institutional discrimination we encountered. This was 2003. All donations of blood and blood products were tested and retested before they were used. Carl was denied the selfless act of donating his blood and possibly saving a life.

In 2013, gay men were granted the right to donate blood on the condition they hadn't had a same-sex partner in the last five years. I wondered how many gay men were actually eligible blood donors as a result of this policy change. Heterosexuals, bisexual females, and lesbians could have endless sexual partners and their donations were welcomed. But a gay male was only allowed to donate if he had never had a same-sex partner and to continue donating blood he must remain celibate for the rest of his life. Someday soon, we'll look back at this policy in disbelief.

SHARON ↲

Among the first people I came out to with the news Carl was gay was a young woman who a few years before had had a summer job with me. When we worked together, Sharon got to know Carl and Paul as fourteen- and eleven-year-old boys. She loved them and they loved her.

Sharon was in her late twenties, married and eager to start a family of her own. We had lunch on campus in one of the largest and noisiest cafeterias. It was a convenient place to meet and it was likely we would find a place to sit down. Both of us brought our own lunches to avoid the disappointment of cafeteria food. I told her about my new job and that Carl was living in residence in downtown Toronto. She told me about her new job and that she and her husband would like to build a house in the country and were looking at floor plans. We caught up on parents, nieces, and nephews — her sister had quadruplets, so it was always fascinating to hear about how that family was managing. I visited their home when the babies were eleven months old. All four were awake and crawling around the living room, literally taking the room apart. They had taken every cushion off the couches and unplugged all the lamps. One was eating the soil from a potted plant, another one was turning the dials on the CD player, another one was sitting beside the coffee table tearing up a magazine stuffing paper into his mouth, and the last one was trying to open the door to go outside. The parents were lucky to have a large extended family available to help on a daily basis. The babies' room looked like a highly organized daycare with bins and labels on everything. It was fascinating to hear how her sister and brother-in-law got the two older children dressed, fed, and out the door on time for school. Having caught up on life, it was time to update Sharon on one last piece of information about my family. Even though it was well over a year since Carl had come out I would still tear up when I told people. I had to brace myself and not cry in the packed cafeteria.

My friend and colleague Johnny Linville, who was the manager of horticulture at the High Line, a reclaimed elevated railroad that has been made into a public park in New York City, explained my watershed moments of tears by saying that emotions, like fear, are temporary, but, crying and sadness may happen every time I say "Carl is gay." He asked me to visualize a glass filled with red water and said that was emotion I had inside. If I poured a quarter of the liquid into a glass filled with clear water and added clear water back into my glass, the redness would fade. If I continued to dilute by sharing, eventually the original glass of water would only have a tinge of red. It would become easier the more I shared and let out what was in my mind.

With this analogy in mind I bit my bottom lip and said, "Carl is gay."

Sharon showed no surprise, disbelief, or shock. She sat there with her hands on her lap, paused a second or two, and moved her lips to one side of her mouth. "I think this is more of an issue for your generation," said Sharon. It had about the same impact on her as if I would have told her that Carl was moving into a new apartment closer to campus. Her non-reaction reaction was such a relief.

In the context of my experiences as a teenager and young woman,

Sharon's casual assurances were almost unimaginable. I cautiously took comfort in learning Sharon's generation thought otherwise.

Within a few months of lunch with Sharon, the same-sex marriage legislation became a front-and-centre debate in the House of Commons and in households, schools, and the media across Canada. The ugly battles over the legislation and parliamentary vote resulted in the resurgence of openly expressed and intense homophobia of prior decades by a small but nevertheless vocal and organized segment of the Canadian population.

In spite of the homophobic time baby boomers grew up in, many of us have done a pretty decent job of raising our kids to be largely accepting and supportive. Paul, a genuine people person who recognized all fourteen hundred kids in his high school and knew most of them by name — along with thousands more students at U of A and Ryerson — said that being homophobic is what's frowned upon now, not being gay. In Canadian society, for many, it's no longer acceptable to be homophobic or make casual homophobic comments. It's taken decades to get here and young people believe we're never going to go back.

II

BECOMING PART OF THE COMMUNITY

CARL CAME HOME FROM YUY ONE EVENING AND TOLD ME THE GAY AND Lesbian Community Centre of Edmonton was closing its doors. All I could think was, if this happens it's going to be a catastrophe.

I emailed Kris to find out what was going on. He said that they'd had the same board for decades, and that they were tired and stepping down.

There were a lot of people concerned about what the closing would mean and the board and community were going to talk about the future and disband the current organization at the upcoming annual general meeting.

Carl and I went to the meeting, which was held in a small performance hall in the downtown Unitarian Church. We sat with a dozen YUY kids and the facilitators. Most of the thirty or so people in the room were gay men in their late fifties and sixties.

Many people spoke. One of the founders of GLCCE was a man who had regularly opened his downtown home in the 1970s for gay men to meet and socialize without fear of violence. GLCCE was established because of his initial courage, and sustained because of his ongoing commitment. The original board had been involved for thirty years. It was time for a new group of people to step up and take over the leadership.

I waited until everyone had spoken before I raised my hand. I stood and passionately urged new people to come forward for the good of the young people sitting in the room as well as all the other LGBT kids in the city. "Carl lives for YUY. Sixty kids pack the meeting room every Saturday night. Some of them have nowhere else to go. His dad and I would have been lost without PFLAG. You made straight parents feel welcome. We're all in this together. Where are all of the other support groups going to go when you close? All of you have done a great job getting this far; it's time for others to step up to keep things going. You can't shut the place down and walk away." The YUY kids cheered and applauded and I sat down.

The members voted to disband GLCCE and one of the YUY facilitators led the initiative to put together a new board with the mandate to create a new LGBT support centre. At the meeting an outgoing volunteer was given the responsibility of recruiting, strong-arming if necessary, new volunteers to fill executive positions. Three of four key positions were filled but no one put their hand up to be the treasurer. The outgoing volunteer walked over to our side of the room, looked me square in the eyes, and said, "You don't have to be a member of the community to volunteer for an executive position."

Feeling like I didn't have any choice in the matter I said, "Okay, I'll do it."

My earliest memory of standing up for others happened in grade two. The village school my brother and I attended was part of the regional Catholic school system in a predominantly Catholic area of rural Saskatchewan. There was no public school available for children from the one Protestant family that lived in the area. Our teachers and the school administrators were Order of St. Ursula nuns. Sister Irene, our teacher for grades one through three, routinely strapped students for offences such as wetting their pants. This happened frequently because the little children were afraid to ask to go to the bathroom.

One morning Maria, a shy girl in grade three who was from a farm family where the children and parents hardly spoke English, was crying when she got off the school bus. "Why are you crying?" I asked.

"Lorie makes fun of me," said Maria, gasping for breath between sobs. Lorie was a mean girl who regularly picked on other kids. I was seven years old and decided to confront Lorie, who was a year older than me. To make matters worse she was Sister Irene's niece. Lorie was already off the bus and nearly at the school steps as I ran across the schoolyard to catch up with her.

"You made Maria cry," I said, out of breath. "Stop making fun of Maria and stop teasing everybody." Lorie looked over her shoulder and smirked as she walked up the steps to the classroom door. I ran back to Maria, who was standing alone in the schoolyard. Together we slowly walked to the girls' cloakroom. Later that day I knew I was in trouble when Sister Irene told me to follow her to the back stairwell that led to the basement of the schoolhouse where she strapped children. At the first landing she turned to face me. I stood motionless in the doorway.

"Tell me what you said to Lorie this morning," said the nun.

I thought, this is it — she's going to strap me. I had nothing to lose. I told her that Lorie teases everybody all the time and made Maria cry when they were on the bus.

Irene came back up the stairs and walked me over to the washstand. A bar of soap sat half submerged in a pool of water in a soap dish next to the metal basin. The basin had stagnant grey and brown streaked cold water in it for the students to wash their hands in after they went to the bathroom. The air was thick with the smell of school issue institutional soap and dirty water. I got off with the minor punishment of washing my mouth out with the filthy bar of slimy soap as Irene stood over me watching. For the rest of the afternoon I had gritty flecks of soap stuck to my teeth and tongue. If only I had gagged and vomited on her. Had that happened Irene most certainly would have strapped me, but it would have been worth it. Lorie didn't stop.

Other times I became involved because things needed to change and I was determined to at least try to be part of a better solution. I liked being around people who cared and wanted the world to be a healthier place for everyone. I became involved in women's issues because there were countless things girls weren't allowed to do in the 1960s. In 1969, when I was in grade ten, the girls circulated a petition to be allowed to wear pants to school. The winter temperatures in central Saskatchewan were often minus thirty degrees Celsius and even colder for four to six weeks each year. We didn't have uniforms in our school but the girls were required to wear dresses or skirts in class covering our legs with leotards that were supposed to keep us warm. Considering the climate, by default girls should have been allowed to wear pants to stay warm. If the power went out we wouldn't miss our refrigerator because we could have kept milk cool outside protected in a cardboard box for six months of the year. All the girls with the exception of two sisters signed the petition. From then on girls were permitted to wear pants to school. As children we understood in order for change to happen we had to gather rational, like-minded people together, get organized, and not give up.

Instantly, I was the interim treasurer as well as a member of the official planning group for what would become the Pride Centre of Edmonton. It was definitely not my intention to become a board member when I accepted the invitation to attend the AGM. I had never set foot in the community centre. I didn't have a clue what the issues were and knew no one else on the board. I was unknown to the community and with the exception of Kris and Carl everyone in the room was completely unknown to me. I let the passion in the room pull me into an overwhelming project renewal.

As people said goodbye and left, a young woman in her early twenties sat alone on the stairs at the side of the stage. She had her elbows on her knees and her face in her hands. Knowing I couldn't leave I went over and sat beside her, sensing what was coming could take a while.

"Hi."

Looking straight ahead across the room she said, "I wish my mom was like you."

I didn't know what to say.

She came from a small town and her parents didn't want anyone to know she was a lesbian. She could only talk to her mother about it — her father wouldn't talk about it at all. When she told me her name, I realized I knew of her relatives. With no emotion in her voice, still slumped over, she turned her head toward me, telling me I couldn't tell anyone that I'd met her through the gay community. Her family would be upset if it came back to them in any way. My heart was breaking; she was fearful of anything getting back to her parents in the same way I had feared the kids at YUY would call their friends at Scona to tell them Carl was gay. The difference was that I was fearful for my son's safety at school and her parents seemed to be fearful their name would be sullied or their reputation would be contaminated. Her relatives had been benevolent, unsparing community leaders for generations. I had no way of knowing whether her family was fearful, close-minded, uninformed, or possibly genuinely homophobic.

I sometimes see this same young woman at Pride events and on campus. A few years after I first met her, she told me she was fed up with media coverage of the Pride Parade. That weekend, she and her friends had been at the parade and then spent the afternoon and evening at Celebration on the Square in Sir Winston Churchill Square. They had had a great day visiting the displays, meeting friends, and listening to bands play. When she got home she turned on the TV to watch the late night news. The TV coverage of the Pride Parade featured only the drag queens. This didn't represent her or her friends and she wondered why the media always focused only on the outrageous. She was discouraged and tired of being represented by a single, old stereotype.

I called CFRN–CTV and left a message for the news editor to call me. It took five days of back and forth before we spoke to each other. When I was finally able to ask the rationale for their stereotypic depiction of the Pride Parade, I was told that that was the footage they had, so they ran with it. He had four minutes of airtime to fill and that was that. But things have got better since then. Media coverage of Pride Week events is slowly moving away from rehashing cheap thrills and clichés to actual accurate reflection of the diversity within the LGBT community.

Every week for the next eight months four of us met to plan the new group's future. As a newcomer, my participation during the meetings was limited because I needed time to observe and learn. Besides, my primary responsibility was to sign cheques and keep the finances in order.

Honestly, though, there were times when I was made to feel like an outsider as I was clearly in the minority and not part of the group. On two occasions a lesbian on the executive referred to me to as a "breeder." The first time it happened, I didn't even realize what she meant until I thought about it at home. I'm not necessarily up-to-date on pop culture or derogatory slang so it took me a while to realize what she had said. I made excuses for her, telling myself she must have thought she was being funny. When it happened the second time I was caught off guard again. Instead of confronting her I made more excuses and pitied her, telling myself, she's middle-aged. She's had it tough. She's endured discrimination her whole life. But I was frustrated with myself for not confronting her. Referring to heterosexuals as "breeders" was vulgar as well as demeaning.

GLCCE was dissolved and in its place we established the Pride Centre of Edmonton. I had many contacts in the city and helped open doors. We organized meetings and dinners with the chief of police, the mayor, assorted provincial politicians, senior Health Authority officials, and many others to raise the profile of the Pride Centre. We leased new space in downtown Edmonton in a central location a block off Jasper Avenue on 109th Street across from the Alberta Legislature. As previous executives had done before, we too made an unsuccessful application to obtain charitable status. It took years and several attempts for the application to finally be successful. There was no explanation given for the application's denial, leaving us to speculate whether or not Revenue Canada had a particular agenda. Not having charitable status made fundraising more difficult than necessary as there was no easy way to provide a tax receipt for financial donations. We weren't a lobby group. The Pride Centre of Edmonton, the Gay and Lesbian Community Centre of Edmonton, or whatever the name was throughout its history, was a community organization that existed to support all people in need and particularly members of the LGBT community. After eight months of hard work we had the Pride Centre securely constituted and serving the community. I cheerfully passed the treasurer's duties on to a new executive member who was part of the community.

SPOTLIGHT ON THE DRAG QUEENS ⌒

CARL AND I WERE driving home from Calgary when Leonard called saying he was going to operate the spotlight at the Imperial Sovereign Court of the Wild Rose Annual Coronation drag queen show.

I thought to myself, "What? You've agreed to do what?"

Earlier in the afternoon the drag queens had called the Pride Centre searching for someone to operate the spotlight at the Coronation. They had often made donations to the Pride Centre, YUY, and Camp fYrefly, so every effort was being made to find a solution to their production crisis. One of the YUY facilitators called our house to ask if Carl could help out at the show. As he was on the road with me and wouldn't be home for a couple of more hours, Leonard volunteered. From Leonard's point of view there was only one problem: he had never operated a spotlight before. He gathered this was an important competition and didn't want to look like an amateur. He left the address on the kitchen counter so I could bring Carl to relieve him after we came home.

By the time Carl and I got home, I had worked myself into a panic. Based on nothing, having had no experience with drag queens other than seeing a few of them from a distance in the Pride Parade, I conjured up an irrational, freaky, far-fetched notion of where this competition was being held and what kind of event it was. Anything outrageous I'd ever heard or seen about drag queens, which was, essentially, next to nothing, shot into my head. All I could think was, what insanity did Leonard agree to? Knowing nothing about the place where the event was being held, I was sure that, to get to the event, we were going to have to find some seedy alley and walk up a narrow staircase into a dark cavernous room.

We picked up the address Leonard had left at the house and headed across the river. The first unexpected, but pleasant, surprise came when I realized we were driving to the Masonic Hall, one of Edmonton's beautiful protected heritage buildings in the centre of downtown. The hall is a four-storey brick building with buttresses and turrets. It has a small auditorium with an ornate ceiling and elaborate woodwork throughout with a tiny stage framed with heavy red velvet curtains and a balcony that is perfect for a spotlight operator and a few dozen audience members. As we walked through the intimate terrazzo-floored foyer there were men in drag everywhere.

The second pleasant surprise occurred when I recognized a parent from our sons' junior high school who was there watching the competition. I was also relieved there was at least one other woman in the Hall.

The last, biggest, and best surprise was that the event was charming and absolutely nothing like what I had imagined. The drag queens were polished entertainers dressed as women in elaborate costumes. They were engaged in a fun competition that each took seriously. The performers wore exaggerated false eyelashes, makeup, hair extension, wigs, tiaras, veils, spiked heels, false fingernails, and padded bras. One of the drag queens was dressed as Liza Minnelli. The event was a fun party and the entertainers had huge smiles on their faces as they performed for a panel of judges. Leonard and Carl stayed for the evening and worked the follow-spotlight for each performance. Leonard described the experience as being like any other volunteer activity where a father and son were asked to pitch in and help.

I've since spoken with a few drag queens and once saw Darrin Hagen, a high profile Edmonton drag queen, in performance. I have the impression the camaraderie and friendship that happens while getting dressed for the nightly show — putting on all the makeup and accessories and going through the preparations in the dressing room — are a huge component of what goes on with men in drag.

After listening to a few of these men, it struck me how similar their backstage routine was to that of players in hockey locker rooms. When men play hockey they arrive at the rink well in advance of the ice time. They love sitting around the locker room shooting the breeze while getting their equipment on. They play hockey for forty-five minutes and then go back into the locker room where they shoot the breeze some more, have a beer, and go home. When these men were kids, they spent hours goofing around with their friends in the locker room before and after games. As adults, they have a beer, put on their elbow, shin, and shoulder pads, pull their hockey socks and jerseys over their pads, tape and re-tape their sticks, and enjoy friendship and camaraderie. It takes four or five hours to play forty-five minutes of hockey and it takes six or eight hours to go out in drag for a few minutes in front of the spotlight. To me it appears these two activities have a lot in common: a bunch of people get together regularly to have fun. One group enjoys playing hockey while getting a good workout every week and the other group enjoys entertaining while raising significant dollars for charities. Both groups get to spend time with individuals they relate to and feel a sense of belonging.

Since my initial hysterical reaction, I've learned drag queens are generally not transgender as I had thought but are usually, although not exclusively, gay men. I've also learned that the gay community holds drag queens in high esteem for their part in the 1969 riots in New York City where they, along with LGBT patrons of the Stonewall Inn, stood up to the New York Police Department. The Stonewall Inn was owned by the Mafia and catered to the most disenfranchised segment of the gay community. On June 28, 1969 someone threw the first shoe or brick —

it's uncertain which, causing the three-day riot that was the start of the gay liberation movement in the United States.

Judy Garland, a gay icon, was buried on the same day as the Stonewall riot began. The gay community experienced a profound sense of loss and grief when Judy died. Following Judy's funeral in Manhattan, many people congregated a few kilometres south at the Stonewall Inn. The day culminated with the police raiding the Stonewall and the patrons deciding not to take it anymore and fighting back. "Are you a friend of Dorothy?" (FOD) was a code phrase used by gay men to identify each other. Judy Garland played the role of Dorothy in the movie *The Wizard of Oz*. Dorothy had "queer" friends, as did Judy Garland in her personal life.

SPORTS

It took a few years for me to stop tearing up when I said, "My son is gay." From the start, I was afraid he would be a target for harassment and bullying. My fear of the unknown and perceived potential for high school being a breeding ground for rampant victimization was overwhelming in those early months and years. Thankfully, in Carl's case, none of my apprehension about bullying materialized.

Regrettably, this isn't the case in many parts of the world. Prior to the 2014 Winter Olympics in Sochi, Russian President Vladimir Putin and his government moved backwards, passing a bill banning the distribution of any information— which they called propaganda — that says gay and heterosexual relationships are equivalent. LGBT Russians said the ban allowed for open harassment and intimidation. For months leading up to the Olympics, activists around the world called for a boycott of the Winter Games. During U of A's 2014 Pride Week, I attended a panel discussion that examined LGBT issues in varsity and professional sports, focusing on the Sochi Olympics. The panel members consisted of two lesbians who had played college hockey and competitive ringette, a gay college volleyball player who was then a college coach, and a straight former Canadian Football League football player. Carefully crafted questions on the role of politics, boycotts, and team dynamics in athletics and sport elicited two hours of thoughtful discussion based on informed points of view and lived experiences. All four athletes repeatedly said that politics has no place in the Olympics. The Olympics are about sport. Athletes should not be made to take a stand on human rights issues in host countries.

During the first six months of 2014, President Putin's remarks prompted worldwide debate on LGBT human rights issues. North American media and professional sports in the US were in a frenzy when Michael Sam, a US college football player, and Jason Collins, a National Basketball Association player, came out. In the spring of 2014 the St. Louis Rams, a National Football League team, drafted Sam.

A few months later, Andrew Ference, the captain of the Edmonton Oilers hockey team, marched along with Camp fYrefly kids and organizers in the 2014 Edmonton Pride Parade. Several high profile civic leaders and politicians had marched in the parade in the past but this was the first time one of our Oilers participated. Professional athletes have rarely been vocal LGBT supporters, but in this case Ference was front-and-centre. Most importantly, he had the full and public support of the Oilers and the NHL. Although Ference was a straight ally, he demonstrated true leadership by declaring that for him and his teammates on the Edmonton Oilers, "If you can play, you can play."

NHL player scout Patrick Burke started the "You Can Play" campaign. Patrick's brother Brendan, who was a professional hockey player, came out shortly before he died in a car accident when he was in his early twenties. Brendan and Patrick are the sons of Brian Burke, the president of hockey operations for the Calgary Flames. These events brought public attention to the pervasive homophobia existing in amateur and professional sports.

IN MAY AND OCTOBER 2014, Canada deployed over four hundred civilian election observers to Ukraine for ten days. I volunteered, and was selected from a pool of several thousand applicants. I had been to Ukraine once before, in December 2004 when I was a volunteer election observer during the Orange Revolution election when the international community stepped in to oversee the electoral process that had previously been marred by widespread corruption. In May 2014, on the day I arrived in Kyiv, I was surprised when I saw four same-sex couples walking hand-in-hand on Kreshchatyk, the grand street leading to the Maidan, the central square, which a few months earlier had been the scene of violent demonstrations leading to the downfall of the previous government.

Since Ukraine gained independence from the former USSR in 1991 there has been a struggle within the country between those favouring closer ties with the European Union and those wanting closer ties with Russia. In light of Putin's remarks prior to the Sochi Olympics and the Russian ban on distribution of information about gay equality and given the problems Ukraine was having in the southeast with pro-Russian separatists, it struck me the LGBT Ukrainians took a big chance walking down the street as couples. In May the barricades and memorials from the February massacre were still up and there were uniformed military people with rifles throughout the Maidan and in the tent city on Kreshchatyk. It was a week before the May 25 election and although the streets were quiet, it was impossible for me to tell who was on which side of the issues.

A day and a half later I was sent to Lviv oblast, a province in the northwestern part of the country, along with my partner Jaroslav from Toronto. Over four days, Jaroslav and I, along with an interpreter and a driver, drove over one thousand kilometres in and around the city of Lviv and Lviv oblast. This was a major accomplishment given the overall deplorable condition of the roads off the main highways. In addition to keeping my eyes open for election irregularities, I searched for rainbow signs, but did not see anything anywhere. On election day, Sunday, May 25, while the four of us were driving from village to village, I asked our twenty-four-year-old interpreter Mariya if she was familiar with rainbow flags and their use within the LGBT community. She knew what it represented, but said we wouldn't see any such symbols openly displayed in Ukraine.

I told Mariya, our driver Yarema, and Jaroslav that I was writing a book about the experiences I've had as a result of having a gay son. They listened intently. Yarema adjusted his rearview mirror so he could glance back to make eye contact with me while I spoke. No one reacted as we drove on to the next polling station. The next morning, when Yarema came to pick Jaroslav and me up from the hotel, there was a rainbow umbrella in the back seat of the car where I had been sitting. There was no rain in the forecast that day — the sky was absolutely clear.

At one stop during the morning Mariya took the umbrella out of the car and opened it up, commenting, "It's beautiful." No one talked about why there was a rainbow umbrella in the car, but I can't help thinking this was Yarema's way of showing his support and acceptance of the LGBT community. Less than five months later, in October 2015, I was back in Ukraine for another election. That time I was assigned to much smaller cities and remote mountain villages in the oblast of Transcarpathia, situated in the southwest corner of the country. There were no visible signs of LGBT awareness or support in this region either.

PFLAG

MEETINGS ৴

In 1972 a Queens, New York family marched in the Christopher Street Liberation Day March with a handmade poster, held by Jean Manford, that read, "Parents of Gays Unite in Support for Our Children." Shortly after, Parents of Gays (POG) was formed. Around the same time, families in Toronto were meeting under the POG activist group name, which soon after became a support group as well. The Canadian and US movements were independent of one another but shared the name. All Canadian chapters were renamed Parents, Families, and Friends of Lesbians and Gays (PFLAG) in 2003. The movement spread worldwide.

Leonard and I attended three or four PFLAG bimonthly meetings held at the LGBT community centre. The first we attended was a little unusual in that the office door was locked when we arrived for the seven p.m. meeting. The facilitators apologized for not having the key and reassured us a staff member or volunteer would be coming by shortly to unlock the door for our group. When we got tired of standing, we sat on the floor in the hallway and talked about having gay kids. Half an hour went by and no one arrived with a key so we decided to go to a nearby hotel coffee shop to continue the discussion.

We pushed a couple of tables together and quietly talked about intensely personal matters in a noisy public space. An hour earlier I was worried about being seen going into the gay and lesbian centre, suddenly we were in a public place talking about how we felt about having LGBT children. I would have preferred we had stayed on the floor in the hallway where it was private.

The facilitators did their best to keep the meeting going in spite of the loud background noise of a busy coffee shop. Back in the hallway, the female facilitator told us she had a lesbian daughter in her late thirties and the male facilitator said he had a gay son in his early thirties. He said it took him nearly a decade to accept his son after he came out. He regretted his initial response, but knew it was not uncommon and has come to realize that some people need time to feel more comfortable.

Not everyone was ready to join in the discussion. A young man seated beside us told the group his first name and said he was gay. He was quiet for the rest of the evening. Another middle-aged man introduced himself and he too said he was gay. He described himself as an activist and said he thought his daughter was lesbian.

Two months later we went to our second meeting. Thankfully, this time the centre was open. The format for the evening was the same at every PFLAG meeting. We sat in a circle, shared only first names, and gave a coming-out synopsis, usually our own and our child's. One mother, Joan, attended a few meetings and each time said her son was gay and that he plays hockey. She seemed to think it was impossible to play hockey and be gay. She found it difficult to talk to her son, his father, and his stepfather. Anytime she wanted to talk to her son he'd say there was nothing to talk about and she shouldn't worry about him. This wasn't helping her cope. She had not told her best friend her son had come out because the friend was openly homophobic and proud of it. Joan wasn't able to tell her friend to stop making homophobic slurs and couldn't imagine telling the friend her son was gay, which left her with no one to talk to. PFLAG was the only place she could talk about how alone and helpless she felt.

Joan seemed tortured so I suggested she and I meet for coffee one evening. After listening for a little while I told her she was a nice person and that she didn't have to endure her friend's homophobic insults. I assured her she'd feel better when she stopped subjecting herself to the things and people that hurt her. I was bewildered why a parent with an

LGBT child would continue a friendship with someone she described as a homophobe. To be fair to the friend, Joan should have told her to stop making the comments. After all, she could make new friends, but she is the only mother her son has.

I don't know what happened to Joan and her relationships with her son and best friend.

Everyone was welcome at PFLAG meetings. Although most attendees were sincere people looking for support and for whom we felt compassion, there were occasionally awkward or disturbing encounters. Several of the parents were well into their seventies and many had strong religious affiliations. A minister who attended once said she wished one of her children was gay. She didn't offer any further explanation, nor did the facilitators or any of the parents challenge her to explain what she was talking about. What she said left me thinking, why exactly are you here? She seemed to be saying she wanted to be part of the parents of gays club, an asinine comment and not helpful.

One month a burly oil-rig worker came to the meeting. He said he dressed in women's clothing on the weekends and mentioned how hard it was to find women's clothes that fit him. He said there was no possible way for him to talk about cross-dressing with any of his family, friends, or coworkers on the rig, so he came and spent the evening with PFLAG. He sat slumped over in his chair and sounded hopeless and helpless. I don't know if we were able to help him, but at the very least, PFLAG provided a safe place to come for support.

PFLAG was there to help us in those early months by providing a sense of belonging, as we were part of a new, previously unfamiliar community. We quickly felt better merely because we were able to speak with other parents who shared our experiences; they knew how it felt to have a gay child. We were given support and encouragement as we embarked on the coming-out process as a family.

A couple of years later, the president of the Pride Centre invited Leonard and me to be the PFLAG Edmonton contacts. The local chapter hadn't been active for over a year and the executive wanted to make sure straight parents who needed support had someone they could call. The same thing that had happened with the original GLCCE executive had happened with the PFLAG volunteers — they were tired and it was time for someone else to step up. We agreed to be the facilitators. There was nothing better for us than to be able to sit and talk with other parents who could say, "I know exactly what you mean, I feel that way too," or "That's exactly what happened with us." Having experiences validated by people who were in a similar situation was comforting. Together we learned that we were not alone.

While my time as the interim treasurer of the Pride Centre lasted only eight months, our association with PFLAG went on for years. We agreed to have our home phone number and my first name listed on national and local PFLAG and LGBT websites, and in print publications. Every month we facilitated meetings at the Pride Centre. At the national level, through PFLAG Canada, I participated in conference calls with parent contacts from other provinces. Locally, a group of us marched in the Pride Parade every year. Being in a parade is even better than watching a parade. Before the same-sex marriage legislation was passed there were always four or five placard-carrying protestors along the parade route, usually in front of St. Joseph's Catholic Basilica on Jasper Avenue. Once the protestors stopped coming, the parade was a completely positive experience and fun to be part of. We made sure we were beside the YUY and Camp fYrefly floats. We had a banner and wore black T-shirts that had a large rainbow maple leaf and PFLAG logo on them. A big crowd pleaser was a little remote control VW Bus one of our families had decorated with rainbow streamers and a PFLAG banner, which zoomed in and out of the crowd along the parade route. We always had a boom box playing *We Are Family* by Sister Sledge as we walked the route and waved at cheering supporters.

Each year the number of parade entries and watchers grew. There are now representatives from the Pride Centre board of directors and staff, the mayor and city counselors, Edmonton Public School Board trustees, assorted MLAS and MPS, supportive churches such as the United Church of Canada and the Unitarian Church, businesses, unions, an LGBT cheerleading squad, the Edmonton City Police transit bus, and countless other groups and businesses. Everyone is so happy. The marshaling area is one big party where everyone welcomes each other with hugs and smiles. The march is uplifting because thousands of rainbow-clad, smiling people openly celebrate each other for a few hours once a year.

The parade terminates in Sir Winston Churchill Square or off Whyte Avenue. Everyone is invited to an afternoon party, hosted by some of Edmonton's drag queens, where you can meet old friends, people watch, and listen to speeches and entertainers.

I am not a beer drinker, but one of my best volunteer assignments was selling beer tickets in the beer garden area. One year (before the event got really big) Mary, a PFLAG mom, and I were given cash aprons and rolls of beer tickets and instructed to set up a ticket sales table in the beer garden. The square was packed with a few thousand people. There was no way anyone could have known where to buy the tickets so we stood on top of our picnic table for our two-hour, high-traffic shift and said "hi" to everyone as they came by to purchase tickets. A year before, had anybody told me I would be standing on a picnic table at the Pride Parade after-party selling beer tickets, I would have said flat out that it wasn't going to happen. When it did happen it seemed like a perfectly normal thing to do and I had a blast. It was not unlike Leonard's experience as the follow-spotlight operator at the drag queen competition. Both times the organizers needed volunteers, so we volunteered. Marching in the parade was the fun part of our PFLAG commitment, which lasted nearly seven years.

While we were PFLAG facilitators, the mix of parents and friends who attended monthly meetings was fluid. The same combination of people was never together twice. Each month there were usually four to six people who would return a few times and then go on with their lives as we had a few years earlier. In many ways the format and events were predictable and almost routine. We started the evening by making a safe-space comment reassuring the participants they would not be judged and letting everyone know we were there to support each other. Then we introduced ourselves and shared part of our personal circumstances.

Generally, mothers came with their husbands or heterosexual women friends or sisters. The moms were usually the first to speak and they would immediately dissolve into tears, as I had done. A few minutes later they would collect themselves and talk about their circumstances and how it felt to have an LGBT child. On one occasion a mom's friend spoke for her right from the start while she sobbed. The friend explained the sobbing woman's husband refused to come to the PFLAG meeting. He also refused to talk to his son about being gay and he refused to allow his son to bring home the boy he was dating. Newcomer dads generally sat back on the couches with their ankles and arms crossed. When it was their turn to speak they'd say some version of, "I'm cool with it." Always, after a few minutes, it was clear the dads were having similar concerns and needed to talk too. Fathers have the same fears and worries as mothers. They plainly have different ways of expressing and articulating their emotions. When the men were given the opportunity to speak they said the same things as the women: "I'm afraid, I worry." These were confessions I understood, having been there myself.

One evening we were well into the meeting when a fortyish, well-dressed man came in and sat with us. He said he wanted to observe for a while before saying anything. A few minutes later he shyly interrupted and said he was in the wrong group. He thought the meeting tonight was for gay parents with kids. I could, of course, relate: the moment reminded me of my own misreading of the classified ad the first time I sought an LGBT parent support group. The man said, "I just came out to my wife. We've been married for fourteen years. I need help with coming out to my three young kids." We looked around the room at each other.

I told him the Pride Centre had a weekly Men's Coming Out support group and he left to pick up one of his kids from hockey practice. I see this man at least a couple of times a year at various events. One of his kids came out in junior high.

Another dad came to a few meetings alone. Years before, he, his wife, and his children immigrated to Canada from the Middle East. His wife would not accept she had a gay son. Their son was in his thirties, had never married, and was living in Chelsea, a predominantly gay area in New York City. Having a gay son was tearing his family apart. The father wanted to know how he could support his son and he also wanted advice on what he could do to help his wife accept their son. Along with attending monthly PFLAG meetings he had several conversations with Pride Centre staff and went for walks and coffee with one of the PFLAG fathers who volunteered at the centre. Although nothing changed with his wife, he appreciated all the support and made a large financial donation to the Pride Centre that year.

Parents usually came to PFLAG meetings right after their kids had come out. They may or may not have suspected their child was gay before, but most had an inkling. We heard stories about unplanned pregnancies, drug and alcohol abuse, suicide attempts, cruel relatives, school bullying, cutting and self-mutilation, and many other troubles. Former PFLAGers sometimes dropped by to say hello with updates about their kids, some of whom were over forty. Together we worried and shared a common fear for their safety. We wondered if they would be able to live fulfilling lives in a sometimes openly hostile society. Many people wanted a step-by-step guide on how to tell their immediate families and friends. Some, like Leonard and I, were in shock, others, like Joan, the mother whose son played hockey, were in denial. The sooner we came to terms with having a gay kid the quicker we were able to get on with our lives.

While there is no exact guide, I could relate to the desire for a step-by-step approach, because, reflecting on my own experience, I had gone through several steps before feeling comfortable. First I had to believe Carl really was gay; the kissing episode in the parking lot left no more doubts for me. Next, I worried he could never be a happy adult; the telephone conversations with Gerry and Lawrence, two total strangers, gave me hope — I believed them right from the start. Meeting Kris at YUY gave me confidence there were people in the world making things better for teenagers. Keeping the secret for seven months was the worst and nearly suffocated me. As soon as I had my mom and best friends' support I knew I wasn't alone. But even then, I didn't stop crying — it took nearly three years for that to pass. Agreeing to be on the board of the Pride Centre let me experience how it felt to be different from everyone else in the room. They were gay. I was straight. I met and worked with many happy and successful gay people.

Several pairs of University of Alberta and MacEwan University nursing practicum students also attended PFLAG meetings as part of their public health placement rotations at the Pride Centre. The students were exposed to real life experiences where they heard first hand from PFLAG parents, and seniors who had been closeted their entire lives. The students also met fifteen-year-olds who'd been abandoned by their parents and from sex trade workers who'd been raped by family members as children. They also met extraordinarily committed LGBT social activists who tirelessly fought for a better world and equality for all. The students got to try out some of the theories they had learned in the classroom and, most importantly, the placement at the Pride Centre provided a broadened worldview for the young, soon-to-be health care providers.

But it's not possible for every practicum student to volunteer at the Pride Centre, so we looked for other ways to reach junior high, high school, and college students. One initiative provided honest and open first-person testimonials from parent guest speakers in human sexuality courses. I was a guest speaker in many classes and saw how students were impacted. In their evaluations students regularly said that they never thought about what it is like for parents to come out about having a gay child.

It would be useful for parents of gay children, whether or not they are associated with PFLAG, to speak to service organizations such as the Rotary, Kiwanis, Lions, Welcome Wagon, Junior Achievement, Newcomers, Junior League, and Optimist Clubs, as well as school parent councils and local chambers of commerce. Parents who may need help or more information but are unable or reluctant to seek it could benefit from hearing another parent's experience and perspective.

PHONE CALLS ᚛

MY PFLAG CONTACT INFORMATION on websites and in publications clearly instructed callers to contact me after six p.m. But the time-of-day restriction was usually overlooked. They called during the day and often spoke with Leonard. Most callers wanted to talk and have their experience validated. Usually many people immediately felt better, and some wanted to know more about the monthly meetings. But more than half the callers felt best having anonymous telephone conversations and wanted to avoid a group setting. Some people wanted information on resources in the community. People eventually found the types of support that worked best for them. What had worked best for me were the times I could sit in a room with other parents whose experiences I could relate to, the telephone conversations with Gerry, and my meetings with Kris.

A fifty-six-year-old man called and launched into an explanation of how he had just come out to himself. I could tell this wasn't going to be the usual PFLAG call. He told me that he and his wife had moved to Alberta from the US in the seventies and were now living in a small town where he sold cars. He admitted that he had been homophobic, but that after thirty years of marriage had an experience while on a road trip to Arizona. He started telling me about meeting someone in a bar who offered him a back rub for his stiff neck and shoulders. I cut him off — this was a lot of detail. I asked if he knew I was a parent of a gay child and not gay myself. He said he did, but wanted to tell his story, then explained that he and the man had sex and that for the first time in his life he felt complete. I was in tears again.

He asked if I knew of a gay men's group where he could go to meet other men his age. He wasn't interested in the bar scene — he was looking for a mature relationship. I told him I would call a few people to see if I could find information for him. Eventually I was able to put him in touch with Prime Timers, a gay men's social club that met once a month to go out to dinner, concerts, plays, and movies. I felt like I was running Ruby's Dating Service. We had several telephone conversations over the next few weeks. One conversation was particularly challenging because he was taking care of his grandchildren, who were constantly interrupting. He was desperate to talk and the kids wanted a snack. Before learning I had a gay son, I never would have thought I'd be researching social groups for middle-aged gay men, but from the first conversation I had with this man I felt I needed to do something for him. I'm glad he called and glad I could help.

A woman called from Calgary on a Saturday afternoon saying she only had a few minutes to talk. Her husband was running errands with their older children, the eldest of whom was seven years old. She was at home with the baby, who was having an afternoon nap. She called to ask how she could tell her children their thirty-something-year-old uncle, who was in the Canadian military, was gay.

I told her she was lucky her kids were so young because if she, her husband, and her brother were open with the kids they'd grow up with this being absolutely normal, so there likely wouldn't be much need to explain anything. The sooner the brother brought home his partner the better. Embracing the brother and his partner without conditions would result in the children doing the same.

Another woman called seeking advice that would help her daughter's partner come out to her parents. I wasn't sure what to say, as my first impression was this sounded similar to an "I have a friend that has a problem" scenario. I suggested her daughter's partner attend a human sexuality class panel discussion I was participating in at MacEwan University that week. The evening of the class a middle-aged couple was waiting outside the classroom when I arrived. They didn't say hello when I walked up, nor did they make eye contact with me while we waited. When it was time for the class to start, the man left saying he would wait in the car. Inside, another middle-aged woman, who I assumed was the woman who had called me, stood awkwardly at the back of the classroom. She didn't take off her coat and she wasn't taking notes. The class was made up of students in their twenties, so these three stuck out in the group. I assumed they were the parents of the lesbian couple. The parents didn't identify themselves, nor did they ask any questions; they came and left anonymously. It reminded me of how Leonard and I stealthily attended our first PFLAG meeting when we wasted all that energy thinking we needed to hide.

We periodically got calls from straight people whose spouses had come out. These calls stumped me. There was next to nothing available for the straight ex-spouses group.

Two calls stuck out in my memory. The first was when a fellow U of A staff member, who was unknown to me at the time, called for help. He was so sad he could barely speak. He said that his wife had told him and the kids that she was in a relationship with a woman and was leaving them to live with her. The man was worried about what would happen to the kids — they were in elementary school — and about what his coworkers would say. I had nothing to offer and could only listen. He was in his mid-thirties and loved his wife. His world had caved in. He told me about the online chat room he had found for straight spouses. I recommended the one book available on the subject. We met for coffee and talked on the phone several times. A few years later he married a wonderful woman, the children were doing well in school, the family had nice friends, and life was back to normal — that is, a new normal.

Around the same time I got a call from a woman who sounded hysterical when I picked up the phone. "I can't believe my husband's gay and that he's leaving me," she screamed. She was in her late thirties and they'd been married for seventeen years, and she wanted to have children. She was also worried about what people in their small town were going to think. I let her rant for nearly twenty minutes. Not once did she say anything about what her husband must be going through. When I asked how her husband was managing, she erupted. "I'm calling because my life is falling apart — he's moved on to someone else." She seemed to only talk about her. As I listened I worried she could become violent if he showed his face.

Finally, she calmed down a bit and I told her that I knew someone who was going through the same thing as her. I suggested it might be helpful to talk to him. She agreed, so I called my colleague, who immediately offered to give her a call. The two connected and spoke a few times.

PRIDE WEEK PANELS ↭

FOR THREE YEARS I organized panel discussions during Pride Week entitled "Parents in the Closet: The Families' Coming-Out Experiences." The first year I invited parents of gay boys and men to be the panel members. There were two mothers, of which I was one, and two fathers. Our sons ranged in age from sixteen to over forty, making the parents range in age from their early forties to early seventies. The father of the eldest gay son used only his and his son's first names. Throughout the 1990s this man and his wife had worked to promote LGBT awareness, understanding and acceptance in the general public. A decade later they still felt they had to protect their identity to ensure their son's privacy and safety. Mary, the mother of the sixteen-year-old, and I were at the other end of the spectrum. We introduced ourselves using our first and last names, talked about our kids, their friends, their high schools and universities, and were completely out to family, friends, and the community. The fourth member of the panel was Dennis Vriend, Delwin Vriend's father.

In 1991 Delwin Vriend, who was then a twenty-five-year-old lab assistant at The King's University College, a faith-based institution in Edmonton, was fired from his job because he was gay. At the time, the Alberta Human Rights Commission refused his discrimination complaint on the grounds that sexual orientation was not protected under the province's human rights code. With the support of his parents and the Edmonton LGBT community, Delwin took the case to the Supreme Court of Canada. The legal case was closely watched and highly publicized. Many Albertans were unaware employers could still get away with firing an employee based on sexual orientation. Photos and footage of Delwin, his lawyers, and a handful of protestors, who were determined to keep legislation as it was, were frequently in the news. Delwin Vriend became a household name in Edmonton. At times he was treated as a celebrity — even Canada Customs agents recognized him and thanked him for persevering. It took seven years of legal battles until, in April 1998, the Supreme Court of Canada ruled provincial governments could not exclude protection of individuals from human rights legislation on the basis of sexual orientation.

Following the Supreme Court ruling, discrimination based on sexual orientation was prohibited in employment practices. Employers could no longer refuse to hire, promote, or provide equal treatment to someone because of his or her sexual orientation, and employees further gained the right to work in an environment free of harassment. Although the Supreme Court decision took immediate effect in Alberta, it wasn't until thirteen years later, in 2011, that the Alberta government actually rewrote the legislation to explicitly include sexual orientation in the Alberta Human Rights Act.

Given the major impact Delwin had on LGBT rights in Canada, it was an honour to have his parents, Dennis and Ruth, in attendance. Dennis participated as a panel member and shared some of his recollections of the tumultuous time. In the fall of 2014, The King's University College drama students presented *The Laramie Project*, which was written in 1999, a year after the Supreme Court ruling in the Vriend case. Meanwhile, twenty-three years — an entire generation — had passed since Delwin's firing.

The next year, I invited four new parents to participate: a married couple who had two lesbian daughters, one in her late teens and the other in her early twenties; a mother with a lesbian daughter in her mid-thirties; and a mother with a bisexual daughter in her mid-twenties. Until that evening, the father in the couple had talked only with his minister about his daughters' sexuality and was out to no one else. With his teenaged lesbian daughter watching from the audience, he sat leaning with his elbows on the table, his shoulders slumped, every now and then looking up as he spoke to a room full of strangers about an deeply private and personal matter. He worried for his daughters' future and their safety and was especially sad that one of the young women seemed to be coping by being angry at the world. His comments were raw and sincere. The fact he agreed to do the panel took courage. It gave the audience, most of who were gay, the perspective of a parent struggling with the very beginning of his coming out process. I've had countless conversations with gay people who said they had never thought about how their own parents dealt with coming out.

Each year the candid testimonials from the panelists brought out passionate comments and questions from the audience. One evening took an unexpected turn during the question and answer period when a woman, accompanied by her husband and their junior high school-aged son, told the audience about the nightmare they were living through. The week before the panel presentation the woman had called me asking for help to prepare for their hearing with the Alberta Human Rights Commission. Her adolescent son had been suspended from school the year before because he was gay. She and her husband were willing to pay for legal assistance to properly prepare for the hearing. I told her I would contact members of the LGBT community on her behalf and invited her to attend the Pride Week PFLAG panel discussion the following week. I emailed Kris, Julie Lloyd (who was a family lawyer and LGBT Edmonton lawyer), and Murray Billett, a high profile local LGBT activist who was a member of the Edmonton Police Commission, to get their advice. I met with Julie in her office to tell her what I knew about the situation. Kris and Murray said they planned to attend the panel the following week.

The night of the panel the mother sat rhythmically rocking back and forth at the edge of her chair while she fidgeted with her coat buttons. By the time it was her turn to speak she looked like she was going to stand up and scream as her eyes filled with tears. Her voice shook as she blurted out that her son was suspended from grade eight because he is gay. He was in a Christian school that was part of the Edmonton Public School system. Tears started streaming down her face. She had enrolled him there because they had been told it was a place where everyone was welcome and all the children were celebrated. But in grade seven and eight he was bullied constantly. He wanted help, so he told the principal he was gay.

The woman was crying uncontrollably as she told the story. Her husband sat motionless, staring straight ahead, while tears ran down his face. Their son sat hunched over beside his dad, hardly able to look up as he wiped away tears with his shirtsleeve. The audience sat in stunned silence, choked back tears, and waited. The mother became more agitated as she reconstructed the treatment they had endured. The principal told the student she had two relatives who were gay and had both died from it.

"He was thirteen years old. How could she say that to him?" the woman sobbed.

Around the same time as the meeting with the principal, the son told his best friend he had a dream where he retaliated against the bullies, and that there was a gun in his dream. His friend told everyone at school about him retaliating with a gun, but she didn't say it was only a dream until a long time after. The police charged the boy with uttering threats. The family fought the charge and he was found not guilty, but the principal suspended him from school for two days anyway. And then on the second day she turned it into five days. Prior to the initial suspension the parents had decided to enroll their son in a neighbouring school for the fall term, so when the five-day suspension was imposed they withdrew him from the Christian school and put him in his new school.

The moderator that year was a young woman who hosted a talk show on one of Edmonton's cable TV channels. She didn't have the experience to smoothly refocus the audience and continue with the discussion. There was clearly no way to move on with the question and answer period, given the intense emotions in the room. I stepped in, thanked the participants, and invited everyone into the foyer for refreshments. I was drained. I wanted to hide in a corner and weep for the family, but couldn't. I had seventy-five audience members standing around looking like they had been beat up. Each person in the room was forced to remember the bullying they had endured when they were the boy's age. Many of them realized for the first time that their parents might have had the same feelings of hurt and sorrow as the mother of the boy and the father on the panel. At the reception Murray came over to me and said, "It's time to circle the wagons." I introduced Murray to the family and stepped aside to let them talk.

With Julie Lloyd's legal assistance the family took their case to the Alberta Human Rights Commission, who began proceedings against the principal and the Edmonton Public School Board. The Human Rights Commission found the school was negligent in protecting the boy and ordered EPSB to take steps to protect its LGBT students. Nothing happened to the principal, although there was progress at the school board. As of 2011, Edmonton Public had a stand-alone sexual orientation and gender identity policy that applies to all schools and programs, including the Christian-based schools like the one the boy attended. The policy commits "to establishing and maintaining a safe, inclusive, equitable, and welcoming learning and teaching environment for all members of the school community. This includes those students, staff and families who identify or are perceived as lesbian, gay, bisexual, transgender, transsexual, two-spirit, queer or questioning their sexual orientation, gender identity or gender expression. The Board expects all members of this diverse community to be welcomed, respected, accepted and supported in every school." It took until November 29, 2011 for this policy to go into effect.

That same evening, a woman and her mother came over to me during the reception to share their story. The woman was in her mid-thirties and had been in a long-term relationship with her partner. Hearing the panel of parents speak the previous year had given her the courage to come out to her family. She had brought her mother to the panel discussion this year so they could hear parents of lesbians share their stories. Her story confirmed to me I was on the right track with the panels and the parents' testimonials.

In the third year I switched things up again, this time focusing on straight people with an LGBT parent or sibling. The first panelist was an eighteen-year-old young woman whose mother was lesbian; another was a forty-something-year-old man whose father was gay and was still living with his wife; and a brother and sister who had a gay brother in his late twenties. The forty-plus-year-old said he had to learn to touch girls, women, and his wife because he had never seen his parents be physically affectionate.

I spoke with over sixty people to line up twelve panelists over the three years. I would have liked to continue the series to include presentations from straight spouses and LGBT parents with children as well as testimonials from the transgender community, but I decided to stop. It was almost impossible to find panelists who were willing to talk about personal matters in a public forum. I was satisfied with the turnout of around seventy people each year. Several audience members commented they appreciated having an information event on the Pride Week calendar of events.

PRIDE PARADE COVERAGE ✍

FOR THE FIRST TWO years after Carl came out I couldn't even go near the Pride Parade, and before that, it had never occurred to me to go. The third year after he came out I marched in the parade in my role as interim treasurer of the Pride Centre, carrying a small Pride Centre placard. It was a family affair with Carl there again as part of the YUY contingent. The Pride Centre board members were there with their partners and to my surprise I saw familiar faces from work. I loved being in the parade — it was a big, portable party. The next day the *Edmonton Journal*'s coverage of the parade and Celebration in the Square featured a big photo of a drag queen and little else. I called the *Journal*'s city editor to scold him about their coverage. I said there were hundreds of participants on floats and people carrying banners in the parade and asked why he ran a photo of drag queens again. The paper was perpetuating the stereotype gay men are drag queens or effeminate. I didn't give the editor a chance to speak and continued in a calm voice, telling him that while the drag queens had one float, there were many more participants in the parade, such as the Pride Centre board, who were carrying placards advertising the new location. Our conversation was short and to the point. When I gave him a chance to speak he actually sounded like he understood what I was annoyed about. The following year the *Journal* ran a photo of Mayor Stephen Mandel and Anne McLellan, a sitting Member of Parliament and former deputy prime minister of Canada, who were the parade marshals. I called to thank the news editor for the photo and story.

For years, TV and newspaper coverage of the Pride Parade continued to focus on one category of entertainers, the drag queens, which represented an important, but small, segment of the overall LGBT community. The coverage did nothing to educate or expose the general public to the variety of entries in the parade or the spectrum of people who are the LBGT community. I would have been less annoyed if media outlets ran photos accompanied with stories about the role drag queens played in Stonewall and their place in LGBT history. I'm not aware of this happening in Edmonton in the last thirteen years, therefore I continued to write letters to the editor and called the city news desks asking them to run accurate depictions of the event.

For a few years I felt like the local poster parent for families with gay kids. I participated in panels, did TV and newspaper interviews, and marched in the Pride Parade. One morning I was walking through the U of A Students' Union Building and was stopped by a colleague who complimented me on a recent story and photo of Carl and me in a local newspaper. Unknown to me until our conversation that morning, my colleague had a lesbian daughter. We spent a few minutes talking about how she and her family felt about having a gay child. She maintained her family was comfortable with her daughter's sexual orientation and then offhandedly said that there was no problem, so her daughter had to create one. I think she was referring to her daughter not doing well with her studies but I have no way of knowing for certain. I was left feeling confused — was the daughter having struggles with her sexuality that resulted in difficulties with her studies, or was the mother saying her daughter was using her sexuality as an excuse for poor grades? Either way, I sensed the mother was frustrated and wondered how helpful this attitude was for her daughter.

Another colleague I had worked with for five years sent me an email one morning thanking me for my letter to the editor. A few weeks later he came into my office, sat down and said, "Our sons have something in common."

"They're both gay," I automatically responded. I had never met his son, so I had no way of knowing, but I was right. He said his son had come out some time ago and the process had gone well as both he and his wife were accepting and supportive. I wonder what prompted him to disclose on that particular day, as we had often worked together and periodically caught up on how the kids were doing. It made me feel good when he eventually was able to share this with me.

It's impossible to know exactly how what you do affects people's lives. I've been an LGBT advocate and ally because the issues personally affect me. At work I have a rainbow sticker on my door and a little rainbow flag on my bookshelf. The flag is directly over an air vent so it moves slightly when the heat comes on. My hope is these rainbow signs and my public advocacy make it safer and easier for individuals and families to come out.

CARL'S FRIEND JEN CAME out to him one summer afternoon while they sat together on the swing in our backyard. Jen was twenty-four and was not out to her family. She worried about coming out to her parents. She was certain she knew how they would react. Carl told her she should talk to me and Leonard.

When she did, there wasn't much we could say except that we'd be there for her. She had to come out in the ways that were right for her. She had suffered years of relentless teasing throughout elementary school. In junior high school she made solidly supportive new friends who she came out to one at a time in the following years. Carl was one of those friends. She spent years worried and stressed about coming out to the most important people in her life because she was scared she could lose some of them.

Jen's parents and siblings were fine people. They were a close-knit family, supportive, and kind, and were there for each other in every possible way. We all believe we know our own circumstances best. Jen thought her sister and dad would be okay, but she worried about how her mom would react. She was certain one set of grandparents would not be okay with having a lesbian granddaughter. She didn't think her parents would stop helping her with her education or throw her out of the house when they found out. She felt that having a lesbian daughter was not something her mom would believe possible in her family. Jen's mom was a wonderful person who was devoted to her family. She was not driven by religion, stereotypes, or ideology. As far as I can tell, her upbringing and life experience simply may not have prepared her to have a gay child. Her mother often asked when she was going to get a boyfriend. Her dad never mentioned boyfriends. She was sure her sister would be supportive but she had to gather the courage to tell her.

Jen was one of Carl's best friends. Leonard and I often ran into her parents in the neighbourhood when we were out walking our dogs in the off-leash area. I felt awkward around Jen's parents because I knew something important about their daughter that she hadn't told them.

It was two years after first talking to us that Jen came out to her parents. She did it over the phone while she was away on vacation. Right after the conversation with her parents, Jen called Carl. She said that her mom was silent and her dad said nothing had changed and that they loved her. A few weeks later Jen got home from her vacation. Nobody talked about the news. Months later I asked how things were going. Jen said she wanted to talk about it with her parents, but they wouldn't have a conversation.

Eventually, Jen told her parents she would like to get married and have a family. Her mother told her it would not be right to have children. Jen and I have talked about this a couple of times. She wants desperately for both parents to be supportive of the idea she can have children and a family of her own.

There were two important things I learned from this experience. First, my discomfort with knowing something important and personal about Jen, which she hadn't shared with her parents, was irrelevant. It was my responsibility to help her by supporting and honouring what she needed. Second, it reminded me not all parents who have trouble adapting to having a gay child are raging homophobes.

When Leonard and I first attended PFLAG meetings, one of the facilitators said it took him nearly a decade to accept his son. He was open about his personal struggle and the destructive effect it had on his relationship with his son. He admitted he had been homophobic.

Time and again parents ask how it is that I have a gay child. In November 2013, CBC Television's acclaimed science series *The Nature of Things* aired the documentary *Survival of the Fabulous*. Bryce Sage, a young, gay filmmaker, set out to find answers to the questions: How is evolution compatible with homosexuality and gay men? Was I born this way? and, What made me gay?

Sage went to several universities where he met with researchers conducting a variety of experiments on these topics. At the Human Sexuality Lab at Northwestern University in Chicago, researchers were looking for biological explanations to the question, Are people born this way? The researchers conducted two tests on Sage. The first test measured blood flow to his penis as he watched gay and lesbian erotica. The second test looked at the part of the brain where instinctive sexual responses are located, the area where erections come from. As he was shown four-second clips of erotic material, an MRI scan lit up the instinct pathways of his brain.

To try to find answers to *What made me gay?*, Sage went to Brock University in St. Catharines, Ontario to meet with researchers who looked at birth order by analyzing the blood of mothers that have both gay and straight sons. His next stop was at the University of California, Los Angeles, where researchers studied identical twins and how it was that one twin could be straight and the other gay. These researchers examined whether hormones in the womb can influence a genetic predisposition to be gay. Sage then interviewed a neuroscientist in Montana who studied male reproductive physiology and behaviour in animals. This researcher found eight percent of rams exhibited same-sex attraction. At the University of Padova in Italy, Sage met with a researcher who was looking at genetic factors that influence fecundity in women and the influence these same genes had on gay men.

None of the researchers featured in *Survival of the Fabulous* have definitive answers to how and why this evolution has occurred, but the research is fascinating and might help us to understand as we contemplate the question, Why am I gay?

Over and over I've heard, "If that's his choice (to be gay), that's his business." My question is, why would anyone choose to be gay? If LGBT individuals had a choice, why would they choose to be a person who by his or her own existence is routinely harassed, discriminated against, treated differently, and at risk of losing everyone who is important to them in life? Additionally, contrary to what some people fear, exposure to gay people will not cause straight people to convert to homosexuality.

It's not a choice. Take babies, for instance. They do not choose to be left- or right-handed. They are born, usually, either right- or left-handed, rarely fully ambidextrous, and sometimes prefer to use more of one hand than the other. Until recently, in some cultures, including Canada and the US, many children were forced to learn to write with their right hand even if they instinctively preferred to use their left hand. Some right-handers shoot the puck, swing a bat, or golf left-handed. We've stopped trying to convert left-handers to right-handedness. If human beings are born preferring a dominant hand, is it possible that in the same way they could be born preferring the same sex, opposite sex, or both genders for partners?

Part Five

I

HOLDING AND NOT HOLDING
PEOPLE ACCOUNTABLE

TO PROTECT MYSELF FROM HEARING HOMOPHOBIC COMMENTS OR STEREO-
typic gay generalizations when I sensed a conversation was headed in
that direction, I immediately told people my son was gay. I've spent a
decade teaching whenever possible and otherwise holding people
accountable for their uninformed, insensitive comments and flippant
remarks. I have to stop myself from screaming when I hear someone
ask about gay parents, "Which one is the mom?" If it's a couple of
men there is no mom and if it's a couple of women they're both moms.
The first year after Carl came out I avoided teachable moments and
walked away. In many cases, I quickly learned all that was necessary was
a simple explanation.

For example, a parent once asked why her son goes to a gay exercise
class and not a "regular" exercise class. I answered that he goes there
because it's the only time during the week he's part of the majority. For
an hour he's like everyone else in the room. She tilted her head and
paused, then said she had just learned something.

The LGBT community has fought for equal rights every step of the
way in Canada. Less than fifty years ago, homosexual acts were considered criminal offences punishable by time in prison. It took until 1986
to have homosexuality removed from the American Psychiatric Association *Diagnostic and Statistical Manual of Mental Disorders*. In Alberta it

took until 2010 for the billing code used by physicians to no longer classify homosexuality as a mental disorder.

The general public's eyes were opened in the 1980s when the AIDS epidemic outed the gay community. AIDS patients, who were sick and dying, could no longer hide their identity. Broader gay issues became personal, real, mainstream issues as more and more people realized they had gay children, friends, and relatives. Homophobia became something that was being directed toward your child, brother, classmate, close friend, relative, or coworker instead of an anonymous bogeyman.

In 2005 the Canadian federal government legalized same-sex marriage. Same-sex couples are getting married and divorced. Partners and same-sex spouses are covered under company insurance plans. Federal and provincial governments are scrambling to create laws that regulate and protect children of same-sex couples as well as the couples, the rights of known sperm and egg donors, and surrogates.

Kids have playmates and best friends with two dads or two moms. These families attend parent-teacher conferences and watch over their kids at the playground along with the other parents. The woman who is at a prenatal class with a pregnant woman is probably not just filling in because the husband is out of town.

I am encouraged by TV shows that show two men kissing each other and feel a responsibility to have a discussion with coworkers and colleagues who complain it's repulsive and shouldn't be on TV. I feel hopeful optimism when I read engagement, wedding, anniversary, and birth announcements and articles in the newspaper accompanied by photos of happy same-sex couples celebrating their relationships and their families.

BEFORE FACEBOOK, TO STAY in touch with high school friends we had long email distribution lists. I was on one such list with a classmate who periodically emailed corny Saskatchewan jokes — poking fun at the province we grew up in. One day an email arrived in my inbox with "Leaf blower for sale" in the subject line. I opened the email to see a photo of a slight young man dressed in a glittery Toronto Maple Leafs stylized hockey uniform sitting on a patch of grass. I checked the distribution list, comparing the list to other emails he had sent. Our close gay high school friend wasn't on the Leaf-blower list. There was at least one lesbian on the list who received the email. I immediately replied, "This is offensive. I see you've taken John off the list. Did you know you have at least one lesbian on your list? Do you think she noticed you took John off? Do you think she might be wondering if you send lesbian jokes around behind her back? My son is gay. Never send me anymore stupid jokes." He wrote back the next day and apologized, but offered no explanation for taking John off the list. Instead he said that he tells his Indigenous friends "Indian jokes" all the time and they think the jokes are funny. There was no point in continuing the conversation.

WHEN PEOPLE START NEW jobs it's typical to talk about their work experience and background with new colleagues and coworkers. On my first day of work in a new position, during the weekly senior management team meeting, the dean of the faculty, who was my immediate supervisor, asked me to tell the group of five a little bit about myself. I talked about some of my past work experiences on and off campus, and then it was time to mention something on a more personal level. Should I mention my volunteer work with PFLAG? I didn't know anyone in the room and was unsure about disclosing I had a gay son. I decided to mention it, as I would have with any other organization I was involved with. Why should this be any different than saying I was on the costume committee for the Ukrainian dance group? I told the group I had a gay son and was the volunteer director of PFLAG Edmonton. No one reacted or asked any questions, leaving me with the impression this was a non-issue. The dean thanked me and we went to the next item on the agenda.

What I didn't know was that one of the people seated at the table was a devout Mormon. A couple of months later, while sitting in my office, he casually mentioned he had prayed for my son. Reaching into his pocket he pulled out his wallet, flipped it open, and fished out a little card that outlined the official Mormon way to live. "Whenever I'm unsure of life I refer to this card for guidance and direction," he said with genuine sincerity. I couldn't believe what was happening. Until then, he had presented himself as a quiet, soft-spoken man. Now I was trapped in my office with a proselytizing Mormon. Why was he praying for my son? Why was he showing me his rules for life card? He went on to offer me comfort, as he believed my child had given in to temptation and was living a life of sin that required redemption through prayer. There was no stopping him. He thought he was providing me with hope. My son was not a sinner, nor was he perverse. What he portrayed as sensitive and thoughtful comments felt like unsolicited insults. Furthermore, if in his eyes my son embodied weakness, sin, and evil by succumbing to the desires of his flesh, what did that make my husband and me — the people responsible for bringing him into this world? By association, we must be evil as well.

I sat transfixed, thinking, how do I make him stop talking and get him out of my office? He was someone I had to work with on a weekly basis. This was going to require tact. I couldn't scream, "Get out of my office!" As he continued to calmly talk about his reference card I looked at my watch, logged out of my email, collected my notebook and a pen, grabbed my purse, and said, "Since we're done talking about work, you'll have to excuse me. I have a meeting across campus." I put on my coat, walked him to the reception area, and left the building. It felt good to be outside in the fresh air where I could clear my head. I went to the bookstore and bought some chocolate.

Coincidentally, a few days later one of the associate deans, who was also part of the senior management team at the meeting on my first day of work, commended me for talking about my PFLAG work. He asked if there had been any backlash from our colleague, which made me wonder if something had happened with this individual before. I told the associate dean about the wallet reference card and how our colleague had offered to pray for my son's soul. But I said there was no point in talking to the colleague, who I felt was a hopeless case who'd been brainwashed into believing his life is right and everyone else is wrong. I wanted to let this one go.

I could have easily gone to the office of safe disclosure and human rights and filed a formal complaint, as I had not invited him into my office to talk about his religious beliefs. In some circumstances this might be the right thing to do. But in this case, I felt more that my colleague was pathetic and less that I was violated. I also knew there was no hope in trying to make him understand what he was doing was wrong. It would have been as effective as pointing to a puddle on the floor and scolding a puppy.

THE FIRST TIME I heard the phrase *so gay* was in 2004. Carl and I were in the foyer of the Citadel Theatre in downtown Edmonton waiting for the doors to open for the Edmonton premiere of *The Laramie Project* by Moises Kaufman. *The Laramie Project* is a play about Matthew Shepard, a young gay student who was tortured and murdered in 1998 when he attended the University of Wyoming in Laramie, Wyoming.

The foyer was packed with high school students, parents, and members of Edmonton's LGBT community. Carl and I were talking with two of the YUY facilitators when one of the women commented on the damaging use of the phrase so gay.

"What do you mean?" I said.

"People say it all the time," she replied.

"What do you mean?"

"Everyone always says, you're gay, that's so gay."

I had never heard the phrase before. Carl and the two women looked at me in disbelief. They began blurting out more examples as they tried to explain that instead of people saying something is stupid, ugly, dull, weird, uninteresting, ridiculous, unbelievable, different, or whatever else that's negative or critical, people just say "that's so gay" or "you're gay" or "you look gay" or "it looks gay" or "that sounds gay."

"What do you mean everyone? I've never even heard it in my life before this moment."

"My sister is in her thirties. She has kids and says it in front of her kids. She knows I'm lesbian. When I tell her to stop she's dismissive and says, 'I don't mean anything bad, everyone says it,'" said one of the women.

Again, I was in a situation where I didn't believe what I was hearing. No one used this phrase when I was in high school or university in the seventies. These women, who were born in the seventies, told me they couldn't remember a time before people were casually using the phrase as a negative descriptor or insult. Carl said he first heard kids using the phrase when he was in junior high school.

EDMONTONIANS' COMFORT LEVEL WITH winter often depends on how old they are. Sometimes, for up to five months of the year, it can be a winter wonderland for children or an Arctic wilderness for snowbirds, the retirees who travel south to Arizona and Mexico every winter. To help students and staff manage the extended frigid below-freezing temperatures, heated walkways and corridors connect many of the university buildings. My office was off one of the busy corridors on the main campus. There were many couches, chairs, and tables throughout the thoroughfares where students study and relax. On one of those cold winter days a dozen students sat together talking. As I walked by, one of them held up a scarf and said, "He looked so gay in this scarf."

My pulse began to race as I continued walking for a few more steps. I could feel my heart slam against my rib cage. I turned around and went back to the students. "One of you said somebody looks so gay. With a group this size there's probably someone gay sitting right here with you. And it's likely several of you have gay siblings and friends. They're probably feeling really bad because they had to endure this ignorant comment." I couldn't stop myself. They were old enough to know better. Not one of them said a word. They didn't move but stared at me. I turned around and walked backed to my office.

To combat and bring attention to the pervasive use of casual homophobic language, Kris Wells, who by then was at the Institute for Sexual Minorities Studies and Services (iSMSS) at U of A, along with Calder Bateman an Edmonton advertising firm, developed the NoHomophobes.com website. The site, launched in September 2012, tracks the live-time usage of homophobic slurs on Twitter. You can read actual, real-time tweets as well as see instant daily, weekly, and all-time statistical data. The results are chilling. One year after the site went up, in primarily Canada, the United States, and the United Kingdom, *so gay* had been used 4,989,213 times. The day I reviewed the site it had been tracked 3,435 times, and it was only eleven a.m. The word *faggot* had been used 18,260,870 times and 12,986 times that day. It's an award-winning project with shocking statistics and more shocking evidence of the damaging and hurtful conversations LGBT people endure every minute of their lives.

WHEN CARL ATTENDED YUY in grade twelve, he and a few of the other boys around his age convinced Kris and the other facilitators a camp for LGBT kids needed to be created. They argued every group of kids or adults that has things in common and similar interests has a summer camp — the LGBT kids deserved a camp too. In 2004, over a few months,

Kris and his graduate supervisor, Dr. Andre Grace, launched Camp fYrefly, a four-day leadership camp in Edmonton for sixty LGBT youth between the ages of fourteen and twenty-four. Through workshops and guest speakers, participants learned how to develop the resiliency necessary to become change agents in their schools, families, and communities. Carl had attended Camp fYrefly as a camper, pod leader, facilitator, and presenter over four years. In 2005 and 2006 he had a part-time appointment as one of the camp planners in the weeks leading up to the camp. Participating in the camp got better for him each year. He loved Camp fYrefly because it was a safe space he and his friends at YUY had helped create. Young adults were making lives better for all the LGBT people involved with the camp. The campers and adult facilitators didn't want the four days to end; each one wished the way they felt at camp could go on forever. For most it was the first time in their lives they were not the minority. At camp, no one had to explain how he or she felt because everyone shared the same day-to-day reality. The kids mourned the impending end of camp and left dreaming about returning the following year.

From the moment campers arrived, they were encouraged to write "happy notes" — positive messages to fellow campers that were put in a "happy note box" — a Chinese food takeout carton they had personally decorated. The idea was that they would keep the boxes after camp and read the positive notes when they got home, and look back on the messages any time they needed a lift. It was a lifetime gift. The notes were one of many camp highlights for Carl.

One summer, when Carl got home from camp, some friends and relatives were at our house for a barbeque. I love to bake and had made an exquisite dessert. Carl was euphoric from the four days and simultaneously lamenting camp was over. He was eager to read his happy notes and decided to open his takeout carton. As I was clearing away the dishes, bringing out dessert and tea, and herding my family to their chairs, he unfolded the first note. A guest, who was not a random acquaintance but someone who was close to our family and had known Carl his entire life, jumped in and interrupted Carl as if she were reading the note. "You're gay," she said in the tone of a playful insult. She thought she was making a joke and then laughed. Carl didn't read the note, everyone was silent and no one knew what to say. Leonard, the boys, and I glanced at each other. She acted as if she hadn't said anything thoughtless and ignored the uncomfortable silence, chirping, "Time to have some cake." We had dessert and soon after everyone went home. Carl went upstairs to unpack while I cleaned the kitchen.

Around eleven that night a very upset Carl came to me, needing to talk about the comment. Neither of us could figure out why in the world she would have said it. He wanted my advice on what to do. I couldn't think of a word in her defence, especially since she didn't apologize on the spot. We talked. I told him to call her right then — there was no reason to wait until morning — and tell her how he felt. Neither of us was going to be able to sleep.

Carl called to tell her he felt bad about her "you're gay" comment. His strategy was to let her speak until she had nothing left to say. She talked for what felt like a long time. When she had finished her explanation, Carl said it was his turn to talk and her turn to listen. He told her if she were to make such flippant offhanded comments to the people she worked with it could be very damaging. Several times she interrupted, trying to explain, and he calmly reminded her it was his turn to speak. He said he heard these kinds of comments all the time and didn't want to hear them from family, friends, or relatives. She made excuses, and also said she was sorry. Having said what he needed to say, Carl ended the conversation. "We're done. This conversation's over. Good-bye."

On another summer afternoon a friend and I sat in our backyard talking about the kids, vacation plans, and aging parents when I asked how his ninety-year-old mother was doing and whether he was planning a trip abroad to visit her. Gazing at the summer sky he said with a laugh that she was doing well, still following the royals, and "keeping track of who's gay." Sadly, he was not shaking his head about an old woman's pathetic thrills but instead he was making a joke at the expense of gay people. The same moment the words came out of his mouth he realized what he'd said and apologized immediately.

Every fall for years, our longtime close friends invited the same small group to their home for dinner. The group consisted of senior university administrators and their spouses and kids. We'd catch up on the continuing saga of aging parents and, as we got older, started talking about our sore knees. We all looked forward to hearing about what was new with the kids. In 2007 Paul graduated from high school, worked all summer, saved his money, and went to Australia for four months. We told the group it took only a few minutes for Paul to go online, answer a couple of questions, and get an Australian work visa. One of the group interjected, "Did they also ask is your name Bruce and are you a poofter?" Everyone except Leonard and me laughed. When we left we mentioned to our hosts the evening was awkward for us following the joke.

The hostess quietly said that he didn't mean anything.

The following morning I woke up with the comment still reverberating in my mind. I was hurt and kept thinking, he knows Carl is gay, how could he say that? At noon I thought I'd waited long enough for him to call and apologize. This was not a conversation I wanted to delay. I called his home and to my relief he picked up the phone.

"I need to speak to you about what you said last night." Silence. "I don't appreciate you making jokes at the expense of the gay community. It didn't feel very good last night and I had to speak with you when it was still on my mind this morning." In an embarrassed and hushed voice, he immediately apologized.

These three events fall into the category of things we all say that we later regret. I too have said things without thinking that have permanently damaged or changed relationships. I believe these three individuals are LGBT allies. These same people wouldn't even dream of making comments or jokes that could be interpreted as racist or sexist. Unfortunately, injurious and thoughtless comments don't just come from homophobes; at times nice people say things that are hurtful and inappropriate. The incidents have affected our relationships with these individuals. I do not regret that Carl and I held them accountable for their comments but I do regret they felt it was okay to make gay jokes.

FOR A FEW YEARS things went smoothly as I had been spared from opportunities to confront family and friends about their offhanded comments. When I began to relax, I was reminded it's likely never going to end. In 2010 at our nephew's wedding in Nashville, Tennessee it happened again.

Leonard and I arrived in Nashville a few days before the wedding so we could drive to Memphis to see Graceland — Elvis Presley's home — and Sun Studios. Until then I wasn't a big Elvis fan and the only country music star I knew or really liked was Johnny Cash. Touring Elvis's home, his jet, seeing his cars, motorcycles, records, clothes, movie posters, and grave was unexpectedly interesting. His natural smile was beautiful. His handlers developed the cheesy curled-up-lip grin persona. It gave me a new appreciation of the King, who made musical history in my lifetime. We met two loyal fans at breakfast in our hotel who had travelled from as far away as England to see Graceland because they loved Elvis Presley.

Countless rock and roll and country music stars recorded in Sun Studios. We toured the iconic little building, which stands today as it was in the 1950s. It's lined with photos of Johnny Cash, Jerry Lee Lewis, Elvis Presley, Carl Perkins, and many others. We had dry-rub ribs at the Rendezvous Restaurant. The night before the wedding parties began, we attended the IBMA (International Bluegrass Music Association) Awards in the Ryman Auditorium, the original site of the Grand Ole Opry. Carl and Paul and a handful of relatives from around the US flew in. It was the perfect trip.

The wedding day arrived. Our nephew and his fiancée were married in a beautiful little stone chapel at Vanderbilt University. We all went to a local restaurant for wedding cupcakes. For the reception and dance, we had a bird's-eye view of downtown Nashville from the party room in a fancy high-rise condominium.

Our nephew had two groomsmen and a best man. Early in the evening a woman in her forties was dancing with one of the groomsmen. As she passed me on her way off the dance floor, she leaned over, and with her hand at an angle at the side of her mouth, rolled her eyes and said, "I think he's gay."

I shot back, "Oh really. That's great. My son's gay." She stopped, swaying backwards as if she had ricocheted off an invisible wall. I then asked if we should introduce the two men to each other. Her eyes bulged, her mouth was wide open — she couldn't speak. She stared at me for a couple of seconds before walking away. She disappeared and I didn't see her again that evening. I was shaking. I told myself this was a one-off incident. Move on. Enjoy the wedding.

The next morning we were invited to the bride's mother's home. As we walked across the road toward the house I saw two women standing and talking in the front yard. It was the bride's mother and the woman from the night before. I said, "Good morning," as we walked past on our way inside the house. A few minutes later she came into the living room, which was full of more relatives from both sides of the family. As we were formally introduced and shook hands our eyes locked. Neither of us smiled, made small talk, or said a word about our exchange the night before.

I've been on a bit of a mission since Carl came out. I simply don't want to hear anything negative or offensive, and I know it's easy for me to be offended. I'm usually dumbfounded when these things happen, unable to speak. I'm glad I was able to think fast enough to suggest we introduce the young men to each other.

Am I being overly sensitive? I don't think so. In my lifetime homosexuality has been treated as a mental illness, consensual sex between two men was a criminal offence, discrimination on the basis of sexual orientation was one of the last grounds to be added to Alberta provincial human rights legislation, and homophobic comments were socially acceptable to the point where people could make all sorts of remarks and no one would challenge them. The pendulum has swung to the other extreme and has forced people to become mindful of diversity. The use of what in the past was referred to as colourful language could be grounds for harassment complaints and charges.

Giving voice to homophobic opinions perpetuates the socializing of stereotypes. There are many things in this world that are wrong, and it's not okay to promulgate identity-based hate. For several years during Camp fYrefly I was invited to have breakfast with the kids and facilitators on Saturday morning. Following breakfast I always stayed to hear Michael Phair speak to the campers. Michael was a former Edmonton city councilor who was elected to office for five consecutive terms. He was Edmonton's first openly gay politician and is one of our most popular public figures. I've come to know him personally through the LGBT community. He is a wonderful man.

Michael, a man in his sixties, told the group how for most of his life in order to cope he would try to dismiss homophobia by telling himself "people are entitled to their own opinions." Then, one day while he was a guest on a radio phone-in show, a caller was on the line saying awful things. Michael told the caller he had no right to say what he was saying and that he didn't have to listen to him and his hateful comments. Michael told the kids hateful statements do not deserve an audience.

The concept that in order to have a civil society, uninformed beliefs, which lead to negative prejudices, are somehow inherently deserving of respect is flawed. We don't have to respect ignorance, nor do we have to respect a person whose belief system leads to prejudice. Homosexuality is a human condition. A belief system that condemns people for who they are — a system that singles out groups based on ethnic origin, skin colour, gender, religion, sexual orientation, left-handedness, and countless other human conditions, should not be respected no matter how mainstream it may be. In fact, when a belief system is based on hate or ignorance it can't be respected. It is something that should be confronted and condemned. Human beings must be challenged to think about the damage their words and actions have caused. I've learned I'm not obligated to tell people I disagree with them but respect their right to their opinion or belief. It's time we stand up and tell people that some things are simply untrue and unworthy of respect.

II

A Cute Story

A DIFFERENT FYREFLY BREAKFAST INCLUDED AN UNDERCOVER OPERATION TO get a peek at a young couple that wanted to have a baby. I feel so good each time I think about this. Carl came home during an early fYrefly and casually mentioned that one of the facilitators and her partner wanted to have a baby and had asked him to be their sperm donor.

Suddenly, the routine question "How's camp going?" became a serious conversation. I stood motionless to let what he said sink in thinking, okay, quickly get your head around this. Nearly choking, I asked what he told them.

"I said it was nice of them to ask and that it wasn't something I wanted to do at this time in my life."

He had no more to say. I, on the other hand, had a million questions. I was curious to know who the couple was, what they were like, where they were from, what their occupations were, how long he'd known them, how and why they asked him. He could only answer a few of my questions. He knew the facilitator from a previous Camp fYrefly, thought she was from Calgary and about twenty-seven years old.

There was a lot to think about. My imagination was running wild as I pondered the possibilities. Thankfully, I was invited to have breakfast at camp again that year. This was my chance to at least get a peek at what the couple looked like. Luckily, one of them was having breakfast at the same time we were. I didn't need an introduction, as I just wanted to see her. Although she was sitting at a table across the room from us, she was easy to pick out of the crowd because she had black, pink, yellow, and green hair. Apart from the hair, she was conventionally dressed. The fact she had chosen to ask my son to be a possible sperm donor indicated clearly she was an excellent judge of character. It was heart-warming to hear she and her partner wanted to have a baby.

Twenty-one-year-olds usually don't think about donating old clothes to a shelter. Making a sperm donation would have been a serious decision that could only have been made after careful consideration of all of the implications.

That weekend Carl said he didn't think this was something he would ever do because he felt connected to his sperm — it was there for him and not really a commodity. Unfortunately, that didn't help the young women. But I was so proud of his mature response and the thoughtful comments he made afterward. I was honoured the couple would want my son's genes for their child. I'm also very glad my son felt a connection to his sperm, and fully understood there was a potential human being at stake. Still, I couldn't help thinking about the couple and how, had he felt differently or changed his mind, one of them could have been the biological mother of my grandchild.

III

Transgender

As I became more involved in the lgbt community I realized I knew nothing about the "t" group — the transgender community. Early on I asked Carl to tell me what he knew about transgender kids. He was only able to say that it's something that feels right to them.

For several years we billeted kids who came into town for Camp fYrefly. One of my earliest interactions with a transgender individual happened when three fYrefly campers (one lesbian, one gay, and one transgender) were billeted with us. The camp coordinators said the transgender child was male presenting as female and had a gender-neutral first name. The fifteen-year-old I picked up at the bus depot was a boy and he was not presenting as a girl. I had two sons of my own and knew what boys were like. After a few hours at our house with the rest of the campers I was totally confused and wanted to make sure I was using the correct pronoun when I referred to him.

"Which pronoun should I use?" I asked.

He glanced up and studied me. "Awkwarrrrd," he said, in a sing songy voice. Then he added, "He."

As the kids got ready for bed he took off his jacket, then his vest, then a hoodie and a T-shirt. Underneath his T-shirt were bound breasts. I wanted to hold him and cry. At that moment I couldn't believe life could be so merciless. This kid was no different than any of the dozens of kids we had billeted at our house. It didn't matter which sexual organs he had underneath all those layers. He was an almost perfect kid — smart, funny, happy, and he played guitar. But he needed to quit smoking. He deserved to be cared for, loved, and understood. I wanted to protect him and never let him out of my sight. He was a regular kid but already his life was so, so complicated. Simple things like using the washroom at school must have been impossible. If he walked into the boys' washroom he couldn't use a urinal and if he walked into the girls' washroom, the girls would be screaming. Life would get even more troublesome when he tried dating. I felt useless. There was nothing I could do to help except put him to bed, feed him a good breakfast, and drive him to the camp. The next day I let the coordinators know the information they gave me was incorrect.

After a few years I was a little better informed. I'd met more transgender teens and young adults and got to know transgender adults and seniors who were participants on panel presentations with me. Plus, I'd had conversations with PFLAG parents who had transgender children. At a neighbourhood Christmas party my friend told me her adult son, Jim, who I'd known since preschool, was transitioning to female. This was a first for me: a person I had known for most of her life as one gender transitioning to another. I never suspected there was a gender issue with Jim, now Jean.

Compared to the general public, I'd had way more interaction with people who openly identified as transgender. I thought I was comfortable with people in all stages of gender identity, yet something was in my way. I was frustrated with myself and confused with how to think about or refer to our families' shared past experiences when our kids were little. For a year I struggled to understand what was blocking my thinking around Jean's change. All my memories were of Jean as a boy. What could I do with those memories? I couldn't go back and rewrite our history. After a while I realized my attempts to understand were fundamentally flawed. What was happening with Jean was her physical body was being aligned to fit her understanding of who she had been all along. In reality I wasn't remembering a young boy, I was remembering a young girl who, at the time, occupied a body of the opposite gender. That same nice, bright, quiet kid was now a nice, bright, quiet adult. Jean, the person, hadn't changed. She was in the process of doing what felt right for her.

With the dozen transgender people I had met before, I had no past context to adjust to. It was easy for me to accept them as they were. The challenge for me with this group was to imagine how earlier in their lives they had been forced to live in some way as the opposite gender. It was as Lisa, Carl's sixteen-year-old friend, had explained when we met for coffee: when we meet new people we accept them as they are. No paradigm shift is necessary.

The fact that Jean's transitioning was a dilemma for me, the supposedly informed one, underscored how unbelievably difficult life must be for transgender people.

Let's face it, we're all guilty of having been insensitive at one time or another. I attended a human rights conference where author Wayson Choy was the keynote speaker. One of his opening statements was, "We're all a little bit racist." He went on to explain he grew up in Vancouver's Chinatown. His mother, who was a nice person, referred to everyone who was not Chinese as white devils. In spite of the fact that she liked the Ukrainian woman who lived next-door, Mrs. Choy referred to her neighbour as the nice white devil. As he spoke he gave us permission to be human, to recognize unfamiliar territory is threatening and that we sometimes don't adapt as quickly and as fairly as we'd like.

To SUPPORT KRIS WELLS and the staff at Camp fYrefly, Leonard and I drove to Calgary in 2013 to attend the inaugural Pride Week Premier's Camp fYrefly Brunch. It's an easy three-hour drive from Edmonton to Calgary through some of the most spectacular prairie scenery in the country. That morning there was hardly any traffic on the QE2 highway, the sky was clear, and an hour and a half north of Calgary we could already see the majestic Rocky Mountains on the southwest horizon. In this part of the province there are no foothills — it's flat, bald prairie nestled right up to gigantic snowcapped mountains set into the most breathtaking blue sky you will ever see.

Calgary is beautiful. It's set in the foothills with vistas of the Rockies around every corner and the building architecture and public art alone are worth a visit. We took the Memorial Drive exit, drove past the zoo, crossed the glistening Bow River, and parked at the downtown hotel. Former campers greeted and directed us to the ballroom, where a couple of hundred people milled around. Although it was the first Premier's Brunch, Premier Alison Redford was not at the event. We introduced ourselves to the six other people seated at our table and asked what brought everyone to the event. One woman was accompanying a campaigning political candidate and said she'd lived with these issues all her life as she had a gay brother. An hour later, at the end of the brunch program she told us she had two sons, and that when they were young she worried how they would manage if they were gay. But, she said, they were now adults and neither was gay. She added that she also had a daughter who was much younger than the boys and that, because things were different now, she no longer worried whether her daughter would "choose to be gay."

At the use of the phrase, Leonard and I looked at each other. Leonard quietly told me not to bother to say anything — it wasn't worth it. Neither the young gay man who was seated beside me, or the outspoken lesbian senior citizen seated next to Leonard, took the opportunity to inform the woman it's not a choice. I let this one go too as it would not have been polite to single her out in front of five strangers. Nor was it appropriate to invite her to the foyer for a private conversation. The luncheon was over, people were gathering their things and saying good-bye. What she said was not an insult, or mean-spirited. In spite of having a gay brother, she was clueless.

An almost identical comment came from my neighbour a couple of weeks later. Leonard and I were at our annual Labour Day neighbourhood potluck. A neighbour my age told me that most gay people they knew were born that way, and that there were only a few that weren't. This neighbour was a scientist — someone I would have expected to be better informed. I didn't have the energy to continue the conversation by explaining the facts so I excused myself and moved on to the dessert table.

In both these cases the individuals should have known better. I don't know if there will be a time in Carl's lifetime when he will be done coming out. Nor do I know if there will ever be a time when I won't feel compelled to stop an otherwise polite conversation to explain fundamental facts about LGBT issues.

IV

BEING SINGLED OUT

I'VE ALWAYS HAD A LOW TOLERANCE FOR COMMENTS THAT WALK THE LINE between feeble attempts at humour and blatant putdowns. I bristle when I hear references being tossed around about blonde moments, senior's moments, and PMS, to name a few.

In 2012 my job took me to the American Public Gardens Association horticulture conference in Columbus, Ohio. After registration on the first evening, participants were invited to experience some of downtown Columbus by signing up, with other conference participants, for dinner at various restaurants. Whenever Leonard and I have the opportunity we try to support LGBT businesses and we always look for rainbow flags and stickers on business signs and windows. With that in mind I chose the historic walking tour of downtown Columbus, which included a stop at a gay bar, followed by dinner in a restaurant in the gay village. A few minutes before we were to leave I headed to the hotel lobby looking for my group. I spotted a small group of men, one of whom was particularly well dressed, wearing brightly coloured walking shorts with a matching white plaid shirt. I bet this is my group, I thought. Okay, I openly admit I had succumbed to the same kind of stereotyping I am so quick to criticize when I see it in others. But it turns out I was right.

While we waited for latecomers, a man well into his fifties loudly proclaimed to the group, "We have a fag hag with us tonight." Fag hag is a term used to describe heterosexual women who cultivate friendships with gay men. I was the only woman in the group. He was referring to me. I didn't react, but looked at him. Some of the men glanced my way in awkward embarrassment, trying to make me feel welcome instead of singled out as an intruder. For the rest of the evening I avoided the man who made the rude comment.

There were nine of us — eight gay men and me. Our hosts and tour guides were a local couple who loved history. As the evening went by I got to meet and talk with the rest of the group. They were from all over the US and loved plants. Two of the men were the same age as my sons.

The conversation revolved mainly around plants that grow in Zone 3 — a climate classification used to determine the growth capabilities of plants — in western Canada, which for my American companions might as well have been the Arctic. I listed some plants we typically grow including a variety that thrive in my neighbourhood and personal garden such as peonies, lilacs, lilies, ferns, pachysandra, lupins, primulas, elms, mountain ash, oak, tamarack, linden, willows, and more. Everyone participated in the discussion, and there was great interest when I said I have delphiniums and a blue spruce tree, which I learned won't survive in much of the US because it's too warm. Anyone who lives south of latitude 53 is always fascinated by the variety of plants grown way up north in Edmonton.

After a pleasant evening touring Columbus, I resolved the next morning to speak with the man who made the fag hag comment. It was a big conference with over five hundred people in attendance. I had three days to find him in the right time and place where I could tell him how I felt. On my last day, as I was late for lunch, I had to sneak into the banquet room and take the first open seat I could find. I looked to my left to say hello and saw him seated in the chair beside mine. I tried to eat my lunch but my appetite had vanished. I couldn't concentrate on what the keynote speaker was saying. I turned to him and said I needed to speak with him. We quietly left the banquet room, closed the door, and stood face-to-face in the empty foyer. I told him that I'd felt singled out and offended by the way he referred to me on the evening of our walking tour.

He responded that he had assumed I was part of the LGBT community and was making a joke. He stared blankly at me. I told him he didn't know anything about me and that he should never use that phrase to describe any woman again.

He didn't apologize.

I didn't go back into the banquet room, but instead left the lobby and went to my room.

I don't know what motivates people like him. Did he think had I been lesbian I would join in to laugh or sneer at straight women? He didn't appear to understand it's awful to be singled out in a group. It's difficult enough for women to travel alone on business trips. Nowhere in the program material did it indicate the historic tour was for gay men only. He deliberately pointed out I was different and didn't belong, whether or not he assumed I was gay or straight. Even though he had likely endured a lifetime of being singled out and being made to feel he was different and didn't belong, he seemed to have no hesitation in doing the same thing to me.

Johnny Linville, the horticulturist from the New York High Line, was one of the men I met that evening. Johnny admitted that the comment was painful for him, too, but he didn't know what to say, so instead he chose to completely ignore the man and speak to me. It was his way of showing how embarrassed he was.

AFTER CARL CAME OUT he was quick to point out comments that could be interpreted as homophobic, or to confront people who said, "That's so gay." He practically took the head off Paul's fifteen-year-old friend Graham. And then, as time went on, Carl regularly made inappropriate "gay" homophobic comments himself. Maybe Carl thought he was being funny but this really upset his brother. On every occasion Paul was at a loss to know how to handle Carl's comments, which by then had been going on for years. It got to the point where Paul worried about spending time with Carl because of the comments. To Paul it seemed Carl thought he could make mildly homophobic comments because he was gay, but yet he would lash out when other people did something similar.

Carl came home for Easter one year when Leonard and I were away on vacation in Europe. This meant the boys were going to be home together for five days. I could tell Paul was worried about how things were going to go so I emailed Carl to ask that he stop making remarks around Paul and his friends that could be interpreted as homophobic. Carl read the email and immediately called me.

"What are you talking about?"

"You sometimes make comments that, if a straight person made, could be interpreted as homophobic. Paul hates it when you say those things. You've got to stop it." He didn't defend himself or make excuses. Instead, he said he'd talk to Paul.

Carl genuinely didn't know what he had said was so disturbing for Paul, who was also embarrassed because his brother was setting such a bad example. Paul had spent years trying to teach people it was wrong to make casual homophobic slurs. Carl stopped making the comments around Paul and neither has spoken about the issue since. I feel the same way as Paul: the casual homophobic comments made by the LGBT community make me very uncomfortable and I wish everyone would stop it.

I don't know what drives people to say demeaning things about themselves or their peer group. Saying you are appropriating the language doesn't make sense to me. I don't actually believe anyone, LGBT or straight, feels good when the word faggot is tossed around.

When I spoke in human sexuality courses as part of Dr. Brian Parker's panel presentations I told students it's not okay to say "so gay" ever, in any circumstance.

Regardless of the context or tone, I feel exasperated every time I hear the following:

— Which one is the mom/dad, bride/groom, man/woman?
— It's his life ... if that's his choice.
— Most gay people I know were born that way.
— Doesn't matter to me what he does in his own bedroom.
— You worship the devil. I'll pray for you.
— I prayed for your son.
— I don't know how I would react if my son told me he was gay.
— Why didn't you tell me sooner?
— Everyone is entitled to his or her own beliefs and opinions.
— I'm not surprised.

— I would prefer our child to be "this way" than to have cancer.
I know you will agree with me.
— They (gay men) are great houseguests because they're clean.
— You're gay.
— That's so gay.
— I think he's gay.
— She's a fag hag.
— He/she is a breeder.

Part Six

Panels, Politicians, and Safe Spaces

PANELS ⁔

At first i thought i was protecting carl, and myself, by selectively revealing I had a gay son. I surrounded myself with people I didn't need to debate homosexuality with, thereby avoiding situations that were potentially hurtful or could make me angry. Ironically, I found each time I shared my feelings, my fear became less. I went from hiding, to becoming an ally, then an activist, and later a support for other people.

Dr. Brian Parker is a sexologist and staff member at Compass Centre for Sexual Wellness (formerly Planned Parenthood) and a lecturer in human sexuality at MacEwan University and the University of Alberta. His classes range in size from thirty to two hundred students. One of the presentations Brian organizes is an LGBT issues and coming-out panel. For years, as the parent of an LGBT child, I have participated in the panels with individuals who represented gays, lesbians, bisexuals, or the transgender community. At the start of each class Brian asks the students to call out words used to identify the LGBT community. As the students awkwardly respond, Brian fills the blackboard with a litany of demeaning and sometimes hateful jargon. The list includes, but is not limited to, faggot, fag, dyke, butch, fairy, tranny, rug licker, bear, lesbo, poofter, woofter, queer, queen, homo, fruit, shemale, cocksucker and dozens more shocking words and phrases. Often there are words and phrases listed I have never heard. This sets a tone for the class, which in effect says, "We're not going to be dancing around this subject." Next, Brian introduces the panelists and each speaks for about ten minutes. The students always close their laptops within seconds, stop talking and texting, and sit motionless, riveted to the coming-out stories.

When I was part of these panels, I would begin with a quick reference to PFLAG, and then I would ask if there were any students from Strathcona High School in the room. If any hands went up I told the class I was Carl and Paul Swanson's mom. Next I would ask if they knew my sons and then I'd tell them Carl was gay. The presentations were always more difficult for me when there were students in the class who knew the boys. And still more difficult when I recognized students from our neighbourhood or saw my boys' close friends. I knew from experience what I was about to say would make them sad. I didn't have to ask these questions. It would have been easier for me not to know I had a personal connection with some of the students as I always found it easier to speak to a room full of complete strangers, but I also knew that if I could establish that connection with the class I would no longer be a random parent — I would be their classmate or friend's mom.

Testimonials are most useful when people are candid and honest. As panelists we disclosed deeply personal and sometimes private matters. I focused on four main topics: Carl coming out to his dad, brother, and me; the effect keeping a secret had on my soul; Leonard and me telling our parents and their reactions; Carl starting the GSA at school.

Until the winter of 2011, Leonard and the boys had not been to a panel. Carl, although he was living in Toronto and not in Edmonton during the school term, would periodically get Facebook or text messages from friends saying they had heard his mom speak that day. Paul and his girlfriend Danni came to a U of A human sexuality class at eight a.m. one cold winter morning. I knew this was going to be the hardest panel for me to get through because my own child would be hearing how worried and afraid I had been for his brother and him. I asked Brian if it would be okay to have guests in the class and I also got the professor's approval for Paul and Danni to attend. I did not tell the other panel members Paul and Danni were in the class, for a few reasons. First, I wasn't sure when and if they were actually coming. Second, there usually was no time to have even a quick exchange before we got started — we usually talked after the presentations. And, most importantly, I was worried about being able to keep my emotions under control and didn't want to put additional pressure on the other panel members. Participating in the panels was always a huge emotional drain for me because each time it was like repeating my family and me coming out.

At home I had often spoken generally about what I focused on. "I always start with Carl phoning me and coming to my office. I talk about how sad he was about not being able to have kids. I always get a big laugh when I say I repeatedly asked Leonard if he might be gay. Paul's Liberace comment breaks the tension in the room too. Everyone becomes serious when I talk about the damaging effects of secrets, and I close with Grandpa's comment about Uncle Jerry having to hide." Occasionally I'd tell my family about interesting questions or feedback we would get from the students.

Between June 2009 and October 2010 my mother and both of Leonard's parents died. (My dad had died in 1983, before my children were born.) A big part of talking about our family's coming-out experiences focused on how Leonard and I told our parents and siblings Carl was gay. It had been difficult to tell this part of the story after our parents' deaths. The boys knew their grandparents well and loved them. I knew it was going to be even harder for me to get through this section with Paul and Danni in the class that morning because I would have to say Baba, Omi, and Grandpa were gone. I also knew that talking about their reaction would make Paul remember what fine people they were, which would remind him how much he missed them.

The lecture theatre filled quickly. My pulse was racing, my mouth was dry, and my hands were shaking. Even though Paul wasn't going to hear anything he hadn't heard before he was going to be anonymously listening to his mother talk about our family's very personal circumstances to two hundred students. I was doing okay until I got to the grandparents part. Just like LGBT children and adults need their parents' love, understanding, and acceptance, we parents need our parents' love, understanding, and acceptance. As I recalled my phone call to my eighty-two-year-old mom, how she started to cry because I was crying, I had to stop for a few seconds to collect myself before I could continue speaking. I bit my lips together and looked straight ahead, praying I wouldn't start sobbing while I looked out at streams of tears pouring down the innocent faces of at least half a dozen twenty-year-old girls. It was always difficult for me to expose my deepest fears knowing the most useful part of a personal testimonial would leave my family and me vulnerable. It was especially trying to talk about my mom without becoming tearful — she worshipped her grandchildren. From the moment Leonard and I told our parents Carl was gay they showed nothing but support. I am so proud of them; they never let us down.

I always took a minute to speak specifically to the anonymous LGBT students in the classes. I tell them that if they haven't come out to their family because they think their parents will stop paying for their education or make them move out, they have to remain closeted until they finish school. Parents have a responsibility and obligation to provide their children with a place to live and an education. It's too hard for the kids to do all of this on their own so they should try to put up with the secrecy a while longer and get through university.

Along with the personal testimonial I also made a point to tell the students the moment they left the room they were never to use the phrase so gay again. I ended saying, "It's likely most of you will become parents in a few years. Some of you will have gay children. Make it so they are able to come out to you. Your children will need your love and support."

As we walked out of the lecture theatre I asked Paul and Danni what they thought of the panel. Danni said she was expecting the entire presentation to be very depressing and was happy it was positive and informative. Paul said the presenters used humour well to break up intense moments. During the panel he received a text from a new gay friend he had met in first year who was sitting in the same row at the back of the auditorium. The message said, "Your mom is awesome." Paul was struck by the silence in the room, which he described as "attentive quiet" as two hundred students locked in on what I was saying.

A few of us did dozens of panels together. Garrick, a young gay man, while pointing to the body parts he was alluding to, always said, "Girls have a little too much jiggle up here and not enough jiggle down here." He always got big laughs. He came out to his mother when the two of them were in the car driving home from having lunch the last day of summer holidays before his final year of high school. Beth, who initially identified as bisexual and later as queer, came out to herself when she was ten years old. She had dreamt about kissing one of her female friends. As she remembered the dream she realized she liked kissing this girl. Jan, a transgendered man, told a story of serious health problems, including mastectomies as a result of breast cancer. Jan lived with his school-age children, presented as a man and his children still consensually called him mom. Christie, a lesbian, spoke about how she and her wife were painting the fence or doing house renovations. She deliberately focused on and recited everyday chores and errands all of us do routinely in our daily lives. Carol talked about the year she left her teaching job in June as a man and her experiences when she came back to the classroom in the fall as a woman. We had heard each other's stories so often we joked we could do each other's presentations and no one would know.

The most heart-wrenching testimonials always came from the transgender representatives. After the first couple of panels I recommended the transgender person speak last because their testimonials of crippling hardships created an aura of silent trauma in the lecture hall. It was almost impossible to understand how human beings could survive the treatment they had endured. In some cases there had been multiple suicide attempts, hospitalization in mental institutions, severe discrimination, and harassment in the workplace and most had been disowned by their families. They had to struggle to survive. I was shaken by desperate stories. It was almost impossible to believe the speaker had tried to live the first part of their lives as the opposite gender.

At the end of the panel presentation we had a few minutes for questions and then stayed a while longer to speak one-on-one with students. Several times I was asked how Paul felt about having a gay brother, or whether Carl lost any friends when he came out. Once, someone wanted to know if it would have been easier for us if Carl had waited to come out until he was out of high school. This was tough to answer; though I thought it would have been safer for him to wait until university, I didn't have an answer for what the effect might have been for us. A few times there were questions about possibly not having grandchildren. I replied that both Carl and Paul intend to have children. Several times I was asked about sleeping arrangements with boyfriends and I said that in our home the same rules always applied to both children. In fact, the summer between his second and third year of university Carl and I fought for a few weeks about where his boyfriend would sleep when he came to visit. It had nothing to do with gender, but everything to do with our family and all guests in our home. Our sons know it's not who that matters, it's the seriousness of the relationship that's important to their dad and me. At that time neither of the kids was in a serious relationship — no one was living together or engaged. Therefore, no one was sleeping with his boy/girlfriend in our house (at least as far as I knew).

The most frequent one-on-one comments I heard were from the LGBT students who said they wished their parents were more like me and Leonard, or from those who said their parents wouldn't have a conversation with them about being gay. Often, students said they weren't out at home. Sometimes international students and new Canadians would say that in their country they didn't have LGBT people. A few people picked up PFLAG pamphlets wanting information on local meeting dates and times. Many wanted to personally thank us for coming to the class and being open and honest about our experiences.

One particular one-on-one conversation that followed a panel presentation sticks out in my memory. A woman in her thirties came up to me and asked if Carl had ever considered getting a surrogate to have a child for him. I hadn't thought about this much before and wasn't expecting this kind of question. Carl would have been in his early twenties then. I said I didn't think having children was on his mind right then. The woman told me she had carried a baby to term for her aunt and uncle and that she and her husband had two children of their own. "It was easy for me to get pregnant, both pregnancies and deliveries went smoothly. My mother's sister and her husband had tried everything and could not have a baby. Because physically bearing babies seemed to be something I could do easily, I spoke with my mother and my husband and then to my aunt and uncle and offered to carry their fertilized egg and sperm for them. I had their baby for them and am very happy to be able to do this for them."

I asked how she felt when she had to give up the baby. She was entirely pragmatic about the experience, and said she'd known all along that it would be their baby, and it was never a problem when the child was born. This was one of the most selfless and generous acts of kindness I'd ever heard of. I was in awe of this woman. She gave me her contact information and the email address for a national surrogacy group.

I was aware in some cultures it's common for family members to have children for other family members who then adopt the children. In this woman's case the fetus had both parents' genetic material: it was incubated in its cousin's uterus. Recently I told this particular story to an acquaintance, who said it sounded like a horror movie. I disagreed. I thought it was honourable and fantastic.

POLITICIANS ⌁

THINGS WERE GOING WELL. I believed my son was gay. He created the GSA at his high school, had gone off to U of T, and had nice new friends. I volunteered with PFLAG, just like I had volunteered with countless other service organizations throughout my life. Close family members, friends, coworkers, and neighbours were supportive. What could go wrong?

In the early 2000s Canadians began to debate the legalization of same-sex marriage. By 2005 I regularly heard news stories about individuals and groups who opposed changes to marriage legislation. Right-wing fundamentalists wrote anti-same-sex marriage letters to the editor and picketed LGBT centres and pride parades across Canada and the US. The same open homophobia that permeated my high school years was popping up everywhere thirty years later. Everyday protestors spoke out against equal rights for the LGBT community. Unfortunately, what I saw during the long debate brought back the initial fear I had for Carl's safety.

I wanted equality for both my children and became involved in the public discussion on the pro side. Some politicians made anti-same-sex marriage proclamations that they claimed were on behalf of their constituents. It was one day less than a year from when Carl came out to me in my office that I started writing letters to elected public officials about their comments and actions regarding LGBT issues.

What got me started was a statement a few days earlier by David Kilgour, who was then the federal Liberal Member of Parliament for

Edmonton Mill Woods Beaumont. He said if the government made same-sex marriage legal it could lead to legislation allowing mothers to marry their sons. Kilgour, who had been our representative prior to changes in constituency boundaries, made more outrageous statements at a town hall meeting.

I wrote to Mr. Kilgour asking him to support same-sex marriage. Kilgour replied that he was obligated to represent the majority of residents in his constituency, who, he said, opposed same-sex marriage. I wondered how many of his constituents were worried Canada was moving toward passing legislation that allowed parents to marry their children.

At that same time, I wrote to Senator Tommy Banks asking for his leadership and support. The Edmonton senator wrote back denouncing same-sex unions and emphatically stated he would not support the bill. As an unelected senator he didn't even have to pretend he was representing constituents.

This was a huge wake-up call for me. Kilgour had previously had a reputation for being a free thinker and a social activist, especially regarding humanitarian issues in Africa. He had sat in the House of Commons as a Conservative, Independent, and Liberal Member of Parliament. Tommy Banks was a hugely popular and highly respected Canadian musician based in Edmonton who had represented our country around the world. Canadians did want same-sex marriage and equality for LGBT citizens. Both of these men were proven wrong. They weren't representing constituents at all; their responses smacked more of homophobia and political expediency than principle. I tore up both letters and put them in recycling.

SAFE SPACES ↲

When it came time for Carl to pick a university to attend he had only been out for a little over a year. Having him go away from home was a big step for us and an adventure for Carl. Again, I worried about his safety.

Coincidentally, his dad and I were looking at the U of T website at the same time over lunch hour at work one day. We called each other when we noticed there were little inverted rainbow triangles everywhere on the site. It was obvious, and a great relief for us as parents, who were about to send our eldest son off to a big eastern city, that at an institutional level the U of T got it. Their use of rainbow triangles demonstrated the institution recognized there were a variety of people in the world, all of whom were welcome on their campus. When Carl and I visited U of T for orientation that summer it seemed every door had a rainbow sticker on it. It felt so good.

As part of the orientation visit, I made an appointment for us to meet the director of the U of T Safe Space program. The director had arranged for us to be shown around campus by two representatives from LGBTOUT, the U of T student group. Our tour guides were great ambassadors and were particularly proud of the large rainbow triangle chalk drawings they had coloured on the concrete sidewalks throughout campus. The chalk triangles were everywhere and gave me another reason to feel good about Carl going to U of T.

In the late nineties U of T started the Safe Space awareness campaign on its campuses. In the spring of 2005 I felt we needed to do something similar at U of A. I got the idea after Leonard and I saw *Guess Who*, the 2005 remake of *Guess Who's Coming to Dinner*. I was a fourteen-year-old kid in small-town Saskatchewan when I first saw the original movie starring Spencer Tracy, Katharine Hepburn, and Sidney Poitier. In the movie, the Draytons, played by Tracy and Hepburn, were an upper-middle-class white liberal couple forced to confront racism when their adult daughter, who they had raised to be like them, brought home her professional black fiancé, played by Poitier.

I remember talking to my mom about interracial marriage after the movie. We had one distant relative with an African husband who was the first person of colour I had seen in real life, so there was context for us. My mom said she wasn't for or against interracial marriage but thought life would be harder for the couples, mostly because it doesn't happen very often. Forty years later, in 2005, I couldn't believe North Americans were still having trouble adjusting to racially mixed marriages. There had been the civil rights movement, changes in legislation, immigration laws, and better education, but had anything practical actually been accomplished? If you saw *Guess Who* you would be left with the impression nothing had changed. I felt a strong need to ensure LGBT acceptance did not languish in the same way.

The contrast between the institutional support evident everywhere at U of T and the total lack of any LGBT visibility at the University of Alberta prompted me to make an appointment with, Dr. Carl Amrhein, the academic head of the university. The morning after we saw the movie I called to request a meeting. A day or two later, the dean of students returned my call. I told him about the movie *Guess Who*, and about the U of T website and my concern U of A had no visible LGBT support anywhere.

Not long after, I had an eight a.m. appointment with the provost to pitch my idea. I invited Andre Grace, the academic staff member from the Faculty of Education, and his then graduate student, Kris Wells, to accompany me. I had the passion for the issue, they had the vision and strategy. I spoke about our family's relief when we discovered the LGBT-friendly University of Toronto website. We discussed the success Carl had setting up the GSA at his high school. I wanted to make sure Dr. Amrhein understood half the participants at Strathcona High School were allies and LGBT teaching staff themselves. Dr. Amrhein said he was the dean of Arts and Science at the University of Toronto when the initiative was proposed and promised to support this initiative at our institution.

Universities are infamous for moving at a glacial pace. It took over six years to establish a campus-wide Safe Spaces program. There was still little to no obvious LGBT visibility on the U of A website.

II

SAME-SEX MARRIAGE

DURING THE SAME-SEX-MARRIAGE LEGISLATION DEBATE THE ANTI-LOBBY WAS constantly pressing their point, usually using demeaning, condescending language. I attended many rallies and town hall meetings. Sometimes I was the only same-sex marriage supporter in attendance. I would appear to be a solitary, middle-aged woman who blended in with the crowd, but I was immediately the subject of dirty looks when I went up to the microphone to speak. Other times I was part of a small group of PFLAG parents on site with a banner we held high. Often there were other LGBT activists and allies who I recognized and could sit with or stand beside.

Peter Goldring, an Edmonton MP, held a town hall meeting with members of his constituency, a primarily blue-collar neighbourhood in northeast Edmonton. I had met Goldring a few months earlier and had spoken briefly with him when he and I were election observers in Ukraine. He seemed well-intentioned.

Had I known what was on the horizon with Peter Goldring and the same-sex-marriage debate, I would have avoided him. The town hall panel Goldring had assembled consisted of only anti-same-sex-marriage advocates who made no attempt to present a balanced view. The four-person panel included a woman representing Real Women of Canada, a group describing itself as "a pro-family conservative women's movement;"

Link Byfield, the former publisher of *Alberta Report*, a defunct right-wing weekly newsmagazine; former right-wing provincial Member of the Legislative Assembly (MLA) Doug Main; the moderator for the evening; and Goldring. There were no pro-same-sex-marriage representatives on the panel.

Many of the hundred and fifty or so middle-aged and older audience members burst into fits of laughter as the panel members made jokes and mocked gays. They howled with laughter in support of Byfield when he expressed disbelief that a same-sex couple actually felt they were entitled to get married. The gathering felt like a cross between a religious revival and frat party where slick speakers on stage preached to the converted who had come to the meeting seeking validation instead of information. It took enormous willpower for me not walk out of the hall.

When it was time for questions I bolted to the microphone, introduced myself, and reminded Mr. Goldring we had met through election monitoring in Ukraine. Goldring appeared to recognize me and looked happy to have me in the audience. I said I was there to speak in favour of same-sex marriage and that my nineteen-year-old son was gay. Goldring's smile disappeared and his expression quickly changed to dread. "He did not choose to be gay," I said. "We didn't raise him to be gay — this is the way he was born. Most likely everyone in the room has a gay family member." I had everyone's attention. "Give some thought to why they have to hide who they are."

I reminded them that in Canada marriage is bound by civil law. You can be married in your back yard by someone who has the legal authority to marry you, then you can sign the legal documents and you are married. On the other hand, you can have a religious marriage ceremony and not be legally married if the ceremony is presided over by someone who doesn't have the legal authority to marry you.

I told them I wanted my son to have the same civil rights his brother has, to feel that he is valued, to be proud of everything about himself, to choose his partner in life and to marry that person, if he chooses. Finally, I said that my sons did not choose to be right- or left-handed; they were born with one dominant hand. In the same way, my sons did not choose to be gay or straight; one son was born gay.

Goldring said nothing. No one on the panel responded. The moderator didn't thank me for my comments. Everyone in the hall stared at me as I went back to my seat.

Several other members of the gay and lesbian community were in attendance that night and some made it to the microphone to comment. One woman asked the panel why they laughed when Byfield said gays believed they had a right to equal treatment and felt they were entitled to be married. Again, the panel remained silent, not responding to the question. And again, everyone in the room remained silent. It felt like they didn't understand the question. The panel looked at each other and the audience in bewilderment, trying to figure out how to react. They behaved as if we were speaking a foreign language.

At the end of the evening several people, including me, gathered at the back of the hall to talk and support each other. A high school-aged girl stood to the side leaning against the wall. She seemed to be waiting to talk to me, so after most of the people had left I went over to her.

The girl told me she was not out at home or at school, and didn't have anyone to talk to. Her school did not have a GSA. She had been in the hall the entire evening and had heard every word spoken by Goldring and the panel. I felt sick. Then she said, "I'm all alone."

I didn't know what to say. I suggested she give YUY at the Pride Centre a try, if she could get downtown without getting in trouble at home.

It shook me to see a young girl at the town hall; she wasn't old enough to vote and she wasn't out. She took a big risk by simply being in a same room with a hostile group of people, some of whom could very well have known her family. It was also a risk for her to speak with me.

I don't know if she ever went to YUY. Being in a room full of LGBT people who supported her would have been a welcome contrast to the people at the town hall.

A few months later, a man who I recognized as a volunteer from the Pride Centre and who had been at the town hall thanked me for speaking in favour of the legislation that night. He said he was a teacher in Goldring's constituency, in the neighbourhood where the town hall meeting was held, and saw many of his students' parents in the audience. He apologized for not speaking out, saying he was not out at work and couldn't jeopardize his job.

Over and over I've met invisible LGBT community members who were forced to endure open discrimination because it wasn't safe for them to be out. I went through the same fears. It wasn't farfetched for me to have initially worried about losing my job. But it's not just the overt actions that are damaging; the sideways glances I worried about would come to pass.

In 2004 I thought Peter Goldring and I were collaborators in the same cause. It appeared both he and I wanted free and open democratic elections for the Ukrainian people. Watching Goldring in action at the town hall made me suspicious about why he became involved with the Ukraine election situation. Nearly twenty-five per cent of Edmontonians have Ukrainian heritage, including Goldring's wife. Goldring himself had no other ties with the country. Suddenly his involvement in Ukraine and fierce opposition to same-sex marriage smacked of political expediency. In both cases he found what appeared to be popular with his constituents and clung to those issues.

My worst experiences happened at anti-same-sex-marriage rallies organized by local religious groups. One Sunday afternoon several hundred people gathered at the Provincial Legislature, surrounding the giant reflecting pool at the front of the building. Everywhere I looked people were holding signs quoting scripture, denouncing gay people with slogans that ranged from hateful to obscene. Most people there were against same-sex marriage but after hearing word of the rally a few dozen pro-same-sex-marriage supporters had gathered as well. Carl, Leonard, and I were there to make sure PFLAG was visible.

Our sons were in a city choir at that time and across from us, on the other side of the reflecting pool, stood a family from the same choir — Mom, Dad and all six kids ranging in age from three to eighteen years old. Our boys knew two of the kids in this family well as they had taken piano lessons from the same teacher long before they were in choir with each other, plus they had gone on multiple choir trips together over the years. The four kids had been friends for nearly a decade. A Sunday afternoon outing for this family consisted of showing the children it was right to deny a minority group basic human rights by openly discriminating against the LGBT community. They were teaching their children to hate.

Leonard and I joined the small group of pro-same-sex-marriage demonstrators. We picked a spot to stand, while holding our PFLAG banner where we would be out of the wind, near the front and to the side of the Legislature building. A little old nun, probably seventy-five years old, with a scripture reference on a placard, came up to me and said, "You worship the devil. I will pray for you." She wasn't the only one who offered to pray for me. Other Christians came up to me with their hands outstretched, offering to pray for my poor lost soul.

A man confronted Leonard declaring, "Keep your lifestyles to yourself." Leonard shot back, "It's not a lifestyle, it's who you are." The man looked confused and didn't respond. Too many times I've heard similar comments, such as: "Why do *they* need a parade?" and "Why do *they* put their wedding and anniversary photos and birth announcements in the newspaper?" Why? Because gay people are normal human beings who are happy and celebrating milestones and events in their life like everyone else. My interpretation of the comments was, "You can exist, just don't make me look at you." It's sort of like issues of poverty, mental illness, political corruption, food bank use, and Canada's shameful history with Indigenous residential schools, to name a few. There are those that say they can't do anything about it, so they wonder why it is always in the news. It's because important social issues cannot be glossed over, denied, or forgotten. I cared because my son was a target. Through centuries of discrimination and oppression, an LGBT underclass had been created. I had to stand up for his rights and do what I could to change how some people still thought. Civilizations are judged by how they treat their most vulnerable and disenfranchised people. I wanted things to change during my lifetime.

That afternoon at the Legislature we hadn't intended to engage the anti-same-sex-marriage group. Dozens of protestors filed by us spewing venomous comments. Sometimes we couldn't help but respond. The level of loathing and evil in the crowd was so horrifying, and frankly unexpected, that it caused some of the pro-gay attendees great anguish. A PFLAG mother, there with her adult son, completely lost control. She raced up to a protestor and screamed in his face, "How can you be so hateful. This is my son. He's not a sinner. He doesn't hate you, why do you hate him?" She shook with anger and it wasn't hard to see why.

Her beautiful son stood beside her. She was desperate for the people, who reeked with abhorrence, to stop filing past. She wanted them to put their signs away and leave.

Among the placard-carrying, predominantly Christians was a group of about thirty Sikh men with long, greying beards in traditional garb. Their participation was particularly upsetting for us. Not long before, the Royal Canadian Legion had banned turban-wearing Sikhs from their Legion halls, claiming the turbans were essentially hats, which needed to be removed, rather than important parts of religious expression. Canadians had supported Sikh servicemen when they were subjected to discrimination, and eventually the Legion was forced to abandon their policy. In fact, organizations such as the Royal Canadian Mounted Police (RCMP) found ways to incorporate turbans into their uniform code to accommodate religious diversity. Seeing this small group of older men — who we personally had supported in their fight against discrimination — turn around and support discrimination against the LGBT community was discouraging. The same-sex-marriage debate would bring out into the open some of the worst homophobia our country would know, as we seemed to be living through a time when people were eager to openly show how little they knew about LGBT issues.

In a couple of months I transformed from a peaceful rally attendee and observer to someone who wanted to throw punches and tear up banners and placards. Each event pushed me closer to verbal and physical retaliation. By the time I went to my last rally at a park in Mill Woods, an Edmonton suburb, I began to lose control of my temper. Again that day, protesters who seemed to be in a trance offered to pray for me.

At one point a middle-aged man stood in front of me — much too close — and muttered, "I will save your soul." I found his glazed eyes and demonic grin sickening. As he reached to grasp my hand in his religious fervour, I found myself screaming at him not to touch me and calling him a sick human being. I had no control over what was coming out of my mouth. I was shocked by my own rage and knew I needed to get out of there. I passed the banner pole to the woman beside me, headed across the field back to my car, and drove home. I had no experience with verbal assault or physical violence. My mother wouldn't even let us tickle each other when we were kids. I was close to hysteria and had reacted the same way as the PFLAG mother had at the Legislature protest rally. Had the man touched me, I'm sure I would have assaulted him.

The hate I saw at the anti-gay events had infected me. That day I realized it was time for me to stop attending protest rallies and town hall meetings.

In six days I had attended Goldring's town hall, two sessions asking for direction and input on the debate at our local United Church, and a protest rally in the park. At three of the events people who spoke against same-sex marriage had maintained it was the use of the word marriage that was the problem. They supported the traditional definition of marriage, which to them meant a man and a woman. I wrote another letter to the editor pointing out marriage included arranged marriages, common-law marriage, and second and third marriages, and in some cultures polygamy was still practised. Long ago, in North America, marriage ceased to be a lifetime commitment made by one man and one woman. People may be entitled to their own opinions and beliefs but I'm not sure they are entitled to voice these opinions and beliefs when they promote hatred and discrimination toward me and my son or anyone else.

After the vote, legislation permitting same-sex marriage passed and, contrary to the naysayers' predictions, the sky did not fall. Leonard and I continued to get PFLAG phone calls and I facilitated monthly meetings. Time passed and I calmed down again.

III

RELIGION

RELIGIOUS WARS ARE FOUGHT WHERE PEOPLE TORTURE AND MURDER each other based on opposing beliefs. When Leonard and I were the Edmonton PFLAG contacts, easily half of all PFLAG callers, and parents at meetings, talked about the struggles they faced reconciling their religious beliefs with having a gay child. Without exception, being part of a religious community made matters worse for them instead of helping them cope with having an LGBT family member.

Repeatedly, we heard parents say they and their children were not able to be out with their Catholic, Lutheran, Baptist, Christian, Muslim, Anglican, or Jewish parent, grandparents, employers, teachers, relatives, siblings, neighbours, or classmates because of strongly held religious beliefs. The parents' fear of reprisal was often paralyzing and made them hide their children's sexuality, fearful their whole families would be shunned, ridiculed, disowned, or excommunicated.

But how much more stress does hiding cause?

Only a few people were at the point where they had chosen to remove themselves from their religious communities. We assured parents, saying, they and their children were not the problem; the fundamentalists and their lack of understanding were the problem. In my experience this was another example of people being better off removing themselves from situations that are hurtful and damaging rather than trying to fundamentally change themselves to try to fit into a group. For those who were not ready to leave their spiritual home, Leonard and I suggested finding sympathetic and supportive religious leaders and spiritual communities.

Occasionally we heard about congregations and parishes where a minister, priest, imam or rabbi abandoned dogma and interpreted scripture passages such as "You shall love your neighbour as yourself." Matthew 22:34-40 with a twenty-first century perspective. While I was on the executive of the Pride Centre I met LGBT volunteers who were members of Dignity, an organization of Catholics working toward reform as it pertained to LGBT parishioners. Faith and spirituality were significant parts of their lives. They felt they couldn't leave Catholicism and simultaneously felt their church didn't want them. They were able to survive rejection and condemnation by finding individual priests and lay people who welcomed them and included them in their church community.

By the narrow interpretation of a few brief passages in the Bible the leaders of the Catholic Church openly discriminate and promote intolerance toward the gay community. The Church's position on homosexuality — that is, being gay is not a sin unless individuals act on their physical impulses — needs to be reformed. Other issues that could be updated are the increased role of women in the church and re-marriage following divorce. Reform will happen with leadership from the Pope.

Until faith communities officially recognize same-sex marriage and no longer view homosexuality as sinful, people will struggle to reconcile their personal beliefs with doctrine.

I was raised Catholic. As a teenager I liked Christmas caroling with the youth group. My girlfriends and I had fun serving food at wedding banquets the Ukrainian Catholic Women's League catered in our church basement. When I was a little girl I loved playing bingo when my dad was the caller at the Fall Bazaar. But I never connected with the religion and Sunday mass part and I didn't understand sermons. What do "God is love" and "Jesus died for our sins" mean? Penance, and repentance by praying three Hail Marys for fighting with my brother and sister, seemed like a small price to pay. The concept that sins could be worked off through indulgences confused me even more. I never understood what a guardian angel was. In grade one we were taught infants who died before they were baptized were sentenced to eternal life after death in Limbo. Why? (The Catholic Church has since abandoned the concept of Limbo.) So many teachings made no sense to me as a child and even less sense as I grew older and tried to rationally understand religion.

Sister Irene, my teacher for three years in elementary school, frequently strapped the Protestant students in our class because they weren't Catholic. There was no public school for the children of the one Lutheran (referred to as non-Catholic) family who lived near the village school I attended while we lived on the farm. This meant we were all classmates. The rest of us knew Irene deliberately punished the innocent children in the family for something they had no control over. Every day they were made to feel that being Lutheran was wrong and unless they became Catholics they were on the road to hell. In a three-year period Sister Irene had over six hundred days to influence our moral development. The potential for lifelong damage to occur in this classroom was huge.

Apart from Irene, many fine Catholic priests, nuns, and lay people have positively influenced my life. I loved playing badminton with Father Albert, who made learning calculus easy. Brother Bede and Sister Philomena were the embodiment of kindness. Mr. Trach, another excellent math teacher, gave a heartfelt eulogy at my mom's funeral and Father Maurice was my friend.

Literal interpretations of a few select phrases and short passages in the Bible appear to condemn my son for how he was born. Since he is "of me," by association I must be a vile human being as well. As many religious communities do not welcome my son, I don't feel welcome either. Having a gay son gave me another reason to further distance myself from organized religion.

There are church denominations that welcome gay people. Within the United Church of Canada there was a movement in the early 2000s for individual congregations to officially become "Affirming Congregations." For passersby, this meant a rainbow flag would be placed in a visible location somewhere on church property. For the Affirming Congregation it meant their church publicly declared their commitment to inclusion and justice for people of all sexual orientations and gender identities. In 2003 the congregation at St. Paul's United Church in Edmonton, the local church our family had periodically attended, began the process of moving toward becoming an Affirming Congregation.

St. Paul's formed a task force to determine a process for the congregation's input and group discussion. Over the next four years there were Bible study sessions, which examined the context of passages with reference to sexuality. There were organized information sessions, panel discussions, four sermons from the pulpit, and general dialogue in the Church. One particularly informative evening, Dr. Marjorie Wonham presented "Definitions and Acronyms 101 within LGBTTQ." Marjorie was a YUY facilitator and a marine biologist at U of A. This was the third time I had heard Marjorie speak. She defined LGBT terminology including the words gay, lesbian, transgender, bisexual, transsexual, two-spirited, queer, questioning, allied, eunuch, presenting masculine, presenting feminine, intersexed, cross-dresser, drag queen, fetishes, and more. She spoke about the Kinsey Scale, a table from 0 through 6 rating the gradations between exclusively heterosexual and exclusively homosexual behaviour. Marjorie also had everyone do an exercise where we measured the lengths of our index and ring fingers to use as a ratio comparison. Some studies suggest lesbian women have a lower digit ratio than straight women and gay men have a higher digit ratio than straight men. This was an interesting and fun activity that could be tried at home with several straight and LGBT friends for comparison.

At St. Paul's most of the congregation members who attended the presentations had LGBT children of their own. They yearned to have their church and local congregation declare their children safe, welcome, and equal members. Not everyone was supportive. One particularly memorable comment was, "We'll lose all our donors if we become Affirming. Let them (gays) go to Garneau (another university area United Church)." The most vocal opponents were the same people who had tried to organize St. Paul's congregation to oppose ordaining gay ministers in the 1980s.

In May 2007, after several years of deliberation and thoughtful consideration it was time for the congregation to vote on whether to become an Affirming Congregation. For much of its history, St. Paul's congregation votes had been done by a show of hands, but for this issue the vote would be conducted using a secret ballot. Why do we need to hide behind a secret ballot, I wondered.

After a regular Sunday service the congregation was invited to remain seated for a special meeting to discuss the vote. There were many comments from a variety of perspectives during the question and answer period. I remember thinking, which way is this going to go? I couldn't believe what I was hearing.

Much of the discussion was centred on the need to display a rainbow flag at the Church. Many wondered why a visible sign was necessary.

Near the end of the question and answer period Leonard raised his hand to speak. He told the congregation about the anti-gay-marriage rally we had witnessed at the Alberta Legislature. He talked about the people — even children — holding signs saying vile, hateful things about gay people. With the exception of the group of old Sikh men, every person at that rally was part of a contingent from a Christian church. Many Christian churches have sent out very clear messages that gay people are not welcome. Leonard was not worried too much about the size of the rainbow flag, but said we had to have a sign that says to gay people "You are welcome here," because by and large Christian churches are telling gay people they are not welcome.

The congregation voted. Eighty-five per cent of the voters were in favour of becoming an Affirming Congregation. Even though the majority was in favour, I was saddened fifteen per cent — all people I recognized — openly declared intolerance by voting against the motion. Our friends on the pro side, who didn't have gay children, were giddy with the results of the vote. They saw the results as a clear mandate for inclusion. But a majority wasn't good enough for me. I wanted everyone in the room to welcome my son and our family. Only a decade earlier, some of those same people were enamoured with the curly haired little Swanson boy who sang his heart out in the church's children's choir. That afternoon their vote said to the LGBT community, "You don't belong here because we don't accept what you are."

I was not the only one in the sanctuary worried about how the vote was going to go that day. Among others, one of the staff members confided the outcome of the vote would determine whether to pursue a contract renewal. Had the vote gone the other direction, the individual would have felt compelled to leave the congregation, as it would have been impossible to work in an openly homophobic church community.

St. Paul's United Church congregation members and staff marched in the Pride Parade. The church financially supported the Pride Centre and Camp fYrefly and continued to organize LGBT education sessions. In 2009, as part of an Evening Speakers Series, Carl spoke representing Camp fYrefly along with Andre Grace and Kris Wells. An affirming banner and mosaic were proudly displayed in the church and a little rainbow flag was glued on the main front doors. But the congregation decided against replacing the rainbow flag on the sign at the corner of the church lot — for years the flag had been defaced or removed. Instead, the lot sign now has only the subtle official United Church rainbow swoosh identification. It's not a flag, but the message of inclusion is clear.

Overnight the atmosphere in our country changed when the Canadian Parliament legalized same-sex marriage with the passage of Bill c-38 in the House of Commons and Senate in 2005. Dr. Brian Parker of Compass Centre for Sexual Wellness (formerly Planned Parenthood) found prior to the legalization, a high percentage of senior high students would put up their hands saying they disagreed with same-sex marriage. But after the Civil Marriage Act changed to include same-sex couples, only one or two kids in each class would openly oppose same-sex marriage. It could be the students had followed the lead of the majority but by high school, students begin to show signs of independent thought and many have the confidence to act on their own convictions. It helps that people in a civil society respect authority, recognize leadership, and agree to follow general rules of decorum. When our elected officials show leadership and compassion the rest of society will follow.

Part Seven

I

The Pioneers

In edmonton, leonard and i have actively participated in parades, fundraisers, awards ceremonies, seminars, and meetings in the LGBT community. Over the years I've been interviewed, stood on a picnic table selling beer tickets, and supervised young children bouncing around in inflated castles in the family play area at the local Pride Festival. As a result we know many of the activists and socially responsible men and women of all ages at the Pride Centre and in the general LGBT community.

At a Camp fYrefly fundraiser event Leonard sat with a middle-aged community member who immediately asked how Carl was doing. During the conversation she asked, "How long has Carl been happy?" Leonard said Carl has always been happy, like his grandmother, who always tries to focus on the best in life. The question the woman was actually asking was not a question about Carl's inherent personality, but a question about his existence as a young gay man. She has had to be invisible for her entire life. During the day at work this individual is a man with a professional career, while in the evening and on weekends the same person presents as a woman. I think having to do this to survive would be extremely difficult and confusing for most people.

I remembered that when I told my mother about Carl, she replied, "they told me my brother Fred was gay." I never asked who "they" were.

I had already known Fred was gay; when I was in my mid-twenties, my Vancouver cousins had told me. But as he had died twenty years earlier I had never known him, so I wasn't really interested. It never came up as a topic of conversation again. After Carl came out, this part of my family history became much more relevant, and I was curious to learn more about Fred's life.

In 2011 I had visited Pier 21, the Canadian Immigration Museum in Halifax, where I found ship passenger lists and census documents that showed Fedor (Fred/Frank) came to Canada from Ukraine with his parents as an infant when he was less than a year old in 1903. Fred and my mother, Lena, were from a family of thirteen children. My grandfather, Ivan, had five children with his first wife, who died a few years after they arrived in Canada. Ivan then married my grandmother, with whom he had eight more children. Lena was the second youngest and her brother Fred was the second eldest of the thirteen. There was a seventeen-year age difference between Fred and Lena.

Fred was raised on a farm. In Saskatoon he attended Normal School — a place where high school graduates were trained to become teachers prior to the establishment of teachers colleges —but he never went on to teach. He left Saskatchewan when he was a young man and moved to Toronto, where he performed as a female impersonator in vaudeville shows. Some of the family speculated Fred had fallen in love with a woman but it hadn't worked out and he never found another woman. This was a common explanation for bachelor uncles and spinster aunts at the time. In the first half of the twentieth century, Toronto and Vancouver were already large cities where he could live to some degree as a gay man — at least, more comfortably than he would have been able to in rural Saskatchewan.

Fred stayed in Toronto and performed in vaudeville for over twenty years while doing odd jobs on the side. One relative said Fred spent a short time in the US acting in small films playing female parts. After World War II, when he was in his mid-forties, Fred moved to Vancouver where he worked as a waiter in the Busy Bee Café on West Cordova Street. My cousin Stella, who lives in Vancouver and knew Fred well, was eleven years old when he arrived at their home in 1947. Stella said her mother Dora — Fred and Lena's sister — was worried he was going to have a nervous breakdown when he arrived. He had lost interest in life. Uncle Fred slept on their couch in the living room until he found a job and a place to live in a rooming house a few doors down the street from the restaurant where he worked. Slowly, Fred settled into a new life as a waiter. He regularly had Sunday dinner with Dora and her family and left a Gladstone bag in Dora's closet for safekeeping. Every now and then, in private, Fred would add and remove items from the bag.

Fred was a heavy smoker, didn't drink much, and was always nicely dressed and well-groomed. He had a fancy silver cigarette lighter-case combination with his initials, FJS, engraved on it. Fred was in his mid-fifties when he died while reading a book in bed. Nine of the eleven children in my mom and Fred's family and their father died instantly between the ages of fifty-two and early seventies. No one did autopsies in those days, leaving us to believe they had heart attacks due to a congenital heart condition on that side of the family. My mom and a sister lived to be ninety and ninety-six years old, much like their mother who lived to be ninety-two. After Fred died, Dora and Stella opened the Gladstone bag where they found, in Stella's words, "items and articles about homosexuals," which confirmed to them that he was gay.

While researching Uncle Fred I worked with LGBT historians and archivists in Vancouver and Toronto. With the assistance of Ron Dutton, an archivist at Qmunity in Vancouver and Alan Miller at the Canadian Lesbian and Gay Archives in Toronto, we were able to locate information about an arrest that involved Uncle Fred in 1928 in Toronto. Alan spent days searching back issues of *The Globe* and the *Toronto Star* looking for information about Fred and Toronto vaudeville female impersonators between 1920 and 1945.

One afternoon I received an email from Alan, with a scanned newspaper article attached, telling me he found a report in *The Globe* from July 11, 1928 about Fred/Frank and another man being charged with "disorderly conduct" at Cowan Avenue Station. Alan speculated that Fred had been caught in a washroom bust at one of the comfort stations along a streetcar route.

The bust probably wasn't an example of the police calmly writing a ticket and sending the men home. Research on arrests at the time shows the process often included a beating and a night or two in jail, where additional punishment was readily handed out.

When I first learned about the vaudeville performer part of Uncle Fred's life I was excited, because it was a novelty. How many people have relatives in vaudeville shows? Leonard's uncle Jerry was a professional musician, and my uncle Fred was a female impersonator in Toronto — fantastic. The afternoon I received the email from Alan about the disorderly conduct charge, the first thought that came to mind was maybe Uncle Fred and his partner were embracing or possibly walking arm-in-arm and were charged for that. How naive I was to think this. It would have been impossible for two men to openly display any kind of affection in 1928. Gay men had to meet in dangerous places then. Tragically, nearly a century later, in many countries this remains the case.

As I held a photocopy of the newspaper column, a profound sadness enveloped me. There were no gay clubs or bars in Toronto in 1928. When Uncle Fred and his partner wanted to be alone there was nowhere to go. Rooming house owners watched everyone coming and going on their premises, and rooming house walls were paper-thin. They would have been forced to meet in a public washroom. This was my uncle, my dear sweet uncle who, thirty years later when I was four years old, visited us on our farm in Saskatchewan. I was too young to remember him or the visit, but luckily we had an old black and white photo of him with my brother and me.

He was twenty-six years old when the arrest occurred. He escaped rural Saskatchewan to try to make a life for himself in Toronto, three thousand kilometres away. What happened instead was the poor man endured the humiliation of being named in the local paper, singled out as a criminal, for the crime of being who he was.

Carl doesn't have to worry about being arrested for holding hands with his partner while walking down the street in Edmonton or Toronto. Sadly, though, he and his friends have been called faggots on more than one occasion while walking down Bloor Street in downtown Toronto — none of the times were any of the men doing anything to call attention to themselves or provoke name-calling. They weren't even doing something as innocent as holding hands. Drunks on Whyte Avenue in Edmonton have also called Paul a faggot. Whyte Avenue can be an unfriendly place for almost anyone late at night on the weekends.

Leonard has one early memory of meeting his great-uncle Jerry before he died in 1965. In the early sixties when the Lawrence Welk Band appeared in Detroit, the Swanson family met with the band members backstage. Leonard remembers Uncle Jerry as a nice, quiet man but his stronger recollection from that night was of Jo Ann Castle, the exuberant, big-haired, honky-tonk piano player, who talked and smiled and bounced him on her knee.

Leonard's cousin David, who grew-up in California, knew Uncle Jerry well. When the band travelled from Los Angeles — where they recorded the TV series — to Lake Tahoe when performing on the road, Uncle Jerry always stopped in Sacramento to visit his niece — David's mom — and her family. David was fond of Uncle Jerry and said Jerry was a devout Catholic. He remembered reading a letter Uncle Jerry had written to his mom in which he mentioned he had seen a Las Vegas follies show, describing the dancing girls' breasts as resembling fried eggs. David, who was then a boy in his mid-teens, thought this was an unusual way for a man to describe naked women's breasts. Another clue.

Uncle Fred was fifty-five when he died and Uncle Jerry was fifty-four. Our relatives described both men as heavy smokers. Jerry was also a heavy drinker.

FROM MY CONVERSATIONS WITH community members who were over forty-five years old, I learned a disproportionally high percentage of LGBT people have gone through years of anguish, depression, and self-medication with alcohol and drugs. To cope they have had to hide by using deception to protect themselves from a harsh, critical, and damaging society. For decades they've pretended to be someone or something else. Many lives have been lost to suicide because some have found it impossible to carry on.

Over coffee one morning Eric Storey, an Edmonton social activist and highly regarded member of the local LGBT community, said that in order to survive you become extremely good at being invisible, which in turn is very isolating. Eric retired a few years ago after a business career in the manufacturing industry. Following retirement he completed a bachelor's degree in Social Work. For his practicum placement he chose the Seniors Association of Greater Edmonton (SAGE).

For two and a half hours Eric drew parallels between the experiences of gay children in schools and experiences of gay adults in seniors' residences, where peer-to-peer bullying is a way of life. "One of the problems with being an invisible minority is you hear all the comments." People who are racist, sexist, homophobic, bigots, tactless, or plain mean-spirited don't change just because they get old. Sadly, in some cases, these people are more outspoken because they feel they have less or nothing to lose in the latter stages of their lives.

Through his work as a part-time social worker at SAGE, Eric created professional training in queer senior issues that was made available to staff and administrators at seniors' residences and care facilities in the Edmonton area. He created "Bob's Timeline" (see figure) in talks about queer seniors to illustrate some of the deeply ingrained fears and feelings a senior may have. Invisibility, Eric says, plus a different public tolerance of what type of language is acceptable, allowed the closeted to hear very angry, hurtful, and violent language from family, coworkers, and friends. This is one of the major reasons Eric feels so many queer seniors are in a constant state of hyper-vigilance and remain closeted or are so quick to return to invisibility at the slightest perception of non-acceptance.

For his entire career Eric was never out at work. Every day of his life, in order to survive, he still reads the people in the room wherever he goes. In addition to carefully monitoring conversations, he continually scans the group looking for facial expressions, body language, and nuances that tell him whether or not it is safe to be out. A few years before he retired Eric recommended his company's human resources policy manual be updated to include protection of sexual orientation in their hiring policy. The recommendation was denied.

ERIC POINTS OUT THAT queer seniors have spent their lives not being fully honest about who they are as individuals. And there are people who have never had an intimate relationship and now have no one to take care of them in their old age — they have never had a spouse or children. Those who do have kids are afraid their adult children will disown

Bob, born in 1936, is now 76. He finally decided to come out three years ago. Why do you think it took him so long to make that decision?

in	he was	when
1967	31	Everett Klippert was sent to jail indefinitely as a "dangerous offender" for having consensual sex with men.
1968	33	Canada decriminalized homosexuality.
1973	37	The American Psychatric Association (APA) removed homosexuality from its official Diagnostic and Statistical Manual of Mental Disorders (DSM).
1977	41	"Homosexuals" removed from the list of inadmissible classes in Canada's new Immigration Act.
1981	45	More than three hundred men were arrested in police raids at four gay bathhouses in Toronto.
1988	52	MP Svend Robinson of the NDP announced publicly he is gay, becoming the first openly gay Member of Parliament in Canada.
1991	55	Delwin Vriend, an instructor at King's University College in Edmonton, was fired in 1991 for being gay. The Alberta Human Rights Commission refused to investigate the case.
1992	56	Gays and lesbians allowed to enter the Canadian armed forces after a federal court lifts the ban on homosexuals in the military.
1996	60	Bill C-33 was passed, adding "Sexual Orientation" to the Canadian Human Rights act.
2000	64	The Alberta government passed Bill 202 to declare that it would use the Notwithstanding Clause in the event of a court redefining marriage to include same-sex couples.
2002	66	The Alberta government passed a bill to define marriage as exclusively between a man and a woman, and reiterated that it would use the Notwithstanding Clause to avoid recognizing same-sex marriage.
2005	69	Bill C-38, the Civil Marriage Act, passed in the House of Commons in June with a vote of 158–133. The bill formally legalized same-sex marriage throughout Canada. Opposition leader Stephen Harper declared that he would revisit the law if his party should form the next government.
2006	70	A motion to reopen the same-sex marriage debate, tabled by the Conservative government, was defeated in the House of Commons by a vote of 175–123.
2009	73	Sexual orientation is finally written in as a protected ground under the Alberta Human Rights Act.

them if they find out they are gay. Some never learned how to socialize or make friends because they've always had to hide something fundamental about themselves. There is also distrust of the medical system — many among the LGBT seniors population are worried about disclosing they are gay and, as a result, they resist seeking medical attention, which in turn worsens their conditions.

Since 2012, the Over the Rainbow Annual Strawberry Tea has been held at SAGE to celebrate Pride Week and to make it known SAGE is a welcoming and safe space for LGBT seniors. Municipal and provincial elected representatives attend. In 2012 the tea included an official ceremony where Eric and then Edmonton Mayor Stephen Mandel placed a rainbow decal on the front door.

Before getting involved in seniors' issues, among Eric's lifetime of volunteer activities had been his association with Big Brothers Big Sisters where, for thirty-four years, he's mentored children and youth. He has also been a volunteer board member and chair of Big Brothers Big Sisters of Edmonton and Area. When I met with Eric he was a sitting board member of the Alberta Child and Family Services Authority Region 6.

Eric has seen what happens to both straight and LGBT kids whose parents have abandoned them. Some kids try to manage on their own and end up living on the street. Others are in foster care and might be lucky enough to be placed with foster parents who are allies. Big Brothers Big Sisters tries to find adult caregivers for LGBT kids.

EVERY CLASS IN EVERY *School* is the title of a report, published in 2011, on the results of a survey on LGBT attitudes in Canadian schools. A total of thirty-four hundred LGBT students participated in the survey, which looked at a number of topics, including homophobic attacks such as harassment, assault, vandalism, and rumours, and also identified places where harassment and assaults occurred. Students indicated that in order to survive they would plot the route from one class to the next to avoid getting shoved into a locker. They waited until lunchtime to run home to use the washroom. They felt there was no one they could talk to about the harassment because school was not a safe place for people like them.

LGBT youth are bullied, harassed, and physically assaulted more than heterosexual youth — ninety-seven per cent of students in high school report regularly hearing homophobic remarks from peers, fifty-three per cent of students report hearing homophobic comments by school staff, and LGBT youth are thirty per cent more likely to attempt suicide than others their age. A particularly troubling statistic for me, as Carl would like to have children, was that twenty-seven per cent of students who had LGBT parents were harassed because of it. Students in schools with

GSAS felt more supported and were more likely to be open to some extent with peers.

Kristy Harcourt, another high profile Edmonton LGBT activist, has spent her adult life working with sexual minority vulnerable kids. Since 2006 she has been the training and rural development coordinator with the Canadian Red Cross's "RespectED: Violence and Abuse Prevention Program" for the province of Alberta. Kristy says there are countless children who can't think of someone who would help them if they had a problem. She emphasizes that children need an adult to talk to.

For several years Kristy has conducted training sessions for rural bus drivers in small towns across the province to provide strategies for dealing with bullying on the bus to and from school. Adults, she says, have to be courageous because silence is not neutral: it's harmful. In all the years Kristy has worked with young people she has encountered only three families where the parents were outspoken public advocates — the Swansons are one of the families.

Kristy, who has multiple volunteer commitments and usually holds down two jobs, also produces and hosts *Gaywire* on CJSR Radio FM 88, the University of Alberta student radio station in Edmonton. *Gaywire*, which discusses news, events, and issues that affect the LGBTQ community in Canada and around the world, is the longest running show on CJSR and has been on the air since long before Kristy became involved. In 1990, when she was in grade twelve, she walked her dog and listened to the weekly show at six p.m. on Thursdays. At that time mainstream media rarely covered LGBT issues other than AIDS. People fought for change, Kristy says. Several laws changed in the late nineties and early 2000s. Edmonton lawyer Julie Lloyd was a frequent guest on the show. Julie explained changes in the law that applied to the day-to-day lives of the LGBT community, such as partners' rights to power of attorney. The show has evolved with the volunteer producers and hosts. In 2011 *Avenue Magazine* recognized Kristy as one of Edmonton's Top 40 under 40 for the year.

Life for Carl as a thirty-year-old gay man in 2016 is totally different from what gay men and women my age experienced thirty years earlier or what seniors have endured their entire lives. On October 10, 2013

I attended a panel discussion that marked the fifteenth anniversary of *Vriend v Alberta*, in which the Supreme Court of Canada ruled Alberta must include sexual orientation as a protected ground in the province's human rights legislation. One of the panelists said she was born a criminal as she was born before 1969, when homosexuality was removed from the criminal code in Canada. I was troubled by the "criminal" reference and asked Eric, who also had attended the panel discussion, about it the morning we had coffee. Eric recommended I watch the 1961 short film *Boys Beware*, which I was able to find on YouTube. The film was made in the US to warn boys about "homosexual men who may look and sound friendly" (but are really pedophiles). Eric saw this film in elementary school.

Eric knew he wasn't like the homosexuals in the film and thought that one morning he would wake up and like girls.

Eric recounts some of the history of government efforts to weed out homosexuality. In the 1950s and sixties civil servants were given lie detector tests to determine if they were homosexual. In the sixties the RCMP screened applicants using lie detectors. One of the questions they asked was whether applicants were homosexual.

Because homosexuality was a criminal offence until 1969, there is little documented information about LGBT history or activity prior to 1970, when gay men had to hide their personal life. Since decriminalization more of this history is being researched and written about in Canada and the US.

UNTIL THE 1969 STONEWALL riot in New York and the sexual revolution of the sixties and seventies, gay people were treated as sick and deviant. In November 2013 the CBC Television series *Doc Zone* aired *How We Got Gay*. The documentary shows how homosexuality went from being criminalized to medicalized and shows a young man in a psychiatrist's office in the 1950s saying, "I want to change." Doctors, with the consent of parents who believed they had authorized treatment for the good of the child, administered electroshock therapy and induced vomiting as part of a process of behavioural reconditioning. Being homosexual was considered shameful. Boys and men would pray that one day they would be attracted to women. Hotels would refuse to rent rooms to two men, rooming house landlords kept a close watch on who their tenants brought home, and police harassment was constant. Getting caught meant humiliation and personal ruin forcing gay men to perform sex acts in washrooms or public parks, sometimes anonymously. "Lack of understanding and acceptance leads to the creation of a lurid set of myths," said Bob Gallagher of Canadians for Equal Marriage. Gay men hid their identities and sexual relationships because they were forced to hide; they were brainwashed to believe what they were was wrong.

After Stonewall, gays and lesbians had some freedom in protected ghettos, which were established in larger cities across Canada and the US. "Gay Is Good" became a popular slogan. The documentary shows footage from the February 5, 1981 Metropolitan Toronto Police bathhouse raids where 308 men were arrested. A bathhouse is a commercial establishment where gay men can go to have consensual sex and prostitution is not allowed. The facilities usually have some combination of saunas, Jacuzzi tubs, lockers, private rooms, and maybe a swimming pool. Surprisingly, the following day thousands of Torontonians demonstrated in support of the arrested men and against the police, setting in motion the gay power movement in Toronto.

Later that same year, forty gay men in New York and San Francisco were diagnosed with HIV/AIDS. AIDS was another blow to the gay population because they had to endure the initial public perception that a gay person could spread the disease by shaking hands, touching a doorknob, or sitting on a toilet seat. It wasn't until 1996 that the first drugs to save lives were developed and administered lowering the death rate by eighty per cent.

At long last, instead of homosexual activity being illegal, it's against the law to discriminate based on sexual orientation. My sons, their friends, and the YUY and Camp fYrefly kids have grown up in a different and much improved society. In Canada Carl can be himself in just about all situations without the threat of harm. The older generations fought hard for changes in legislation that have set society right, on paper if not always in practice.

II

My Advocacy

In march 2011, edmonton public school board trustees debated and passed a motion authorizing and directing the district to create a sexual orientation and gender identity policy. The evening of the vote a gay high school student, a gay father with children in the school system, and I were invited to speak in favour of the motion as it pertained to our lived experiences within Edmonton public schools. Other members of the LGBT community attended the board meeting to speak in favour of the motion as well.

I outlined how Carl had snuck off to the youth drop-in and his struggle to set up the GSA at Strathcona. I promoted the policy as something that would help students and teachers feel safe, supported, and valued. The high school student talked about the daily bullying he endured, and the gay father told the group he wanted a school system that would protect his children from harassment.

During the following months, as the policy was being drafted, there was significant opposition and controversy lodged by representatives from some Christian schools within the EPSB. Some groups had even threatened to sue the school board.

Many years ago EPSB moved to an open boundaries concept where parents could enroll their children in any public school in the city. Children were not forced to attend their neighbourhood public school and often attended a variety of fully funded, tuition-free specialized programs throughout the city. There are schools specializing in language instruction in French, Ukrainian, Chinese, German, American Sign Language, Cree, and Punjabi, to name a few. We have a fine arts school focused on visual arts, theatre, music, and dance. Sports schools offer competitive athletics, hockey, and soccer training. Academic choices include international baccalaureate and advanced placement programs. There was a full buffet of program and curriculum choices available for families to pick from. Canadian law does not prohibit teaching religion in public schools, so some schools organized to deliver education in a Christian, Jewish, Muslim, or secular environments.

The EPSB gender identity and sexual orientation policy, which ensured the safety and well-being of sexual minority students, staff, and families within Edmonton public schools, was passed in November 2011. In spite of the pushback from some of the parents in faith-based programs, the policy required all Edmonton public schools, including faith-based schools, to adhere to this policy by protecting and respecting sexual minorities.

Carl wasn't bullied in high school or junior high — it helped that he grew to be six feet tall by Christmas in grade eight — but other kids were targeted, and today, kids still are. They hear "that's so gay" dozens of times a day in the hallways and classrooms at school, in shopping malls, at home, and while they're just hanging out. Avram, a twelve-year-old grade seven student in our neighbourhood, said, "Humanity wants to be what society wants them to be. They say it to fit in." He estimated half the kids in his school regularly use *gay* as a put-down to replace words such as *stupid* or *dumb*. No one dares call them out for fear of being bullied, as they would risk being perceived as gay. Kids using the words make sure teachers are not around to hear the language. This shows most students know what they are saying is wrong and hurtful. Avram added, "Kids use words because they hear their parents use the words." At his school there is a campaign in place to stop bullying but Avram said the school board wasn't trying hard enough.

Another reason Carl might have been spared from bullying is because 2003 was a time before every kid had a smartphone. For some kids there is no break. The availability and use of social media has diversified and intensified opportunities for childhood cruelty. Along with worrying about having someone to sit with at lunchtime, an adolescent or teenager's life is made up of constantly checking and instantly reacting to online chatter. Children are marginalized all day long through social media sites, and are mercilessly bullied and harassed for being different. Every month there is a news story about a child taking its own life because of online abuse. None of this is limited to LGBT kids — there are countless potential targets. The most innocent events can be twisted and spun out of control in minutes with a smartphone using photos, videos, and text. This makes it all the more important for schools and school boards, governments, and human rights organizations to have policies and laws in place that provide protection for our children and the general public.

In 1980/81, when Leonard and I were living in New York, I had a freelance job working for the Children's Television Workshop. Every two weeks I'd pick up ten Sesame Street television scripts to condense into five pages of programming highlights. The highlights were distributed to each Public Broadcasting Service station in the US for use in local TV guide listings. I read nearly two hundred Sesame Street scripts that winter and got to know and love every Muppet and human character on the show.

How did a small town girl from Saskatchewan get a freelance job working on Sesame Street in New York City? I sent a letter and my resume to Fran Kaufman, the CTW communications director, asking for an appointment to talk about possible job opportunities. Fran was curious to meet me because I was from Saskatchewan, the home province of Buffy Sainte-Marie, who was a regular guest on the show. Buffy was born on a reserve in the Qu'Appelle Valley, which was a few minutes away from Fort San, where Leonard and I met. I've never met Buffy, but I'm glad the Saskatchewan connection got me an interview and a job on such an influential and groundbreaking television series.

Leonard was born in the US and has had joint Canadian-American citizenship since he was thirty-four years old, so we have closely watched what goes on in America. In 1996 the Clinton Administration and the US Congress passed the Defense of Marriage Act. For the purposes of federal benefits such as income tax and inheritance laws, DOMA determined that *marriage* means only a legal union between one man and one woman as husband and wife. DOMA also determined that states were not required to recognize same-sex marriages performed in other states. On June 26, 2013 the US Supreme Court ruled Section 3, the section that defines "spouse" as a person of the opposite sex in DOMA, was unconstitutional because it violates the rights of gays and lesbians by not providing equal treatment for same-sex spouses under federal laws. The American LGBT community, their allies, and the majority of US citizens rejoiced with this ruling, which expands the recognition of same-sex marriage. Although it's a relief the US is catching up to the rest of the western world, it troubles me progress is so slow in a nation that should be leading the way on issues of social justice.

I have a framed a copy of the July 8–15, 2013 issue of *The New Yorker* magazine on my office wall at work. The cover is the "Moment of Joy" illustration featuring the *Sesame Street* Muppets, Bert and Ernie, where Bert has his arm around Ernie's shoulder as they sit watching the US Supreme Court on TV. The cover of *The New Yorker* connects major experiences I've had during three and a half decades of my life in terms of family and career: my sons and husband have dual Canadian-American citizenship; Bert and Ernie are television characters who reflect the best qualities of human nature; and the United States Supreme Court has moved America forward on LGBT issues that affect our family.

WHAT MADE ME AN advocate and protestor? I saw my mother stand up for what was right when I was an adolescent. My mom worked at the town's seniors' residence on the kitchen, cleaning, and laundry staff for twenty-five years from the time we moved from the farm to town in 1964. The staff at the seniors' residence were paid ten cents an hour less than the staff that did the same work at the town's hospital. Mom took a strike vote petition around for the other staff members to sign. The strike vote passed and the staff threatened to walk out. The threat worked. The women got pay equity with the staff at the hospital, and the staff at the seniors' home joined the Canadian Union of Public Employees. My mother, who always said she didn't like unions, was the shop steward at work and on the negotiating team until her retirement twenty years later.

My mom had guts. The local housing authority operated the seniors' home. The head administrators and spiritual leaders at the facility were the Franciscan Sisters of St. Elizabeth, the same order of nuns that ran the town hospital. In the mid-sixties the entire country was engaged in debates on decriminalizing homosexuality, legalizing abortion, and rewriting divorce legislation. Mom took a petition to work to get signatures in support of legalizing abortion. She believed there had to be a safe place for women to go when they needed to end a pregnancy. All the women that worked at the seniors' home were Catholic farmers' wives, some of whom had eight or nine children each. I can't imagine that the nuns didn't find out about the abortion petition, and I likewise wonder whether any of the seniors added their names to the list. There could have been a serious backlash and my mother could have lost her job, but she did the right thing. Oddly, my mother didn't tell me about menstruation but she openly supported and discussed the need for safe abortions for all women when I was twelve years old.

In MARCH 2014 I attended the Truth and Reconciliation Commission of Canada (TRC) hearings in Edmonton. The TRC was documenting the experiences of survivors and anyone affected by Indian Residential Schools. For more than one hundred years Canadian Indigenous children were required to attend and live in residential boarding schools run by religious orders. In 1966, when I was in grade six, our class went on a year-end field trip to Batoche, Saskatchewan and the Duck Lake Indian Residential School. Batoche is the national historic site that in 1885 was Louis Riel's headquarters and the location of the last battle of the Northwest Rebellion.

I remember a buffalo jump was nearby. Across the prairies Indigenous peoples would stampede buffalo toward a steep embankment, in this case the banks of the South Saskatchewan River, where the buffalo would tumble into a ravine, breaking their legs. The hunters would then kill the animals with spears and knives.

Twenty-five of us white kids, our parent chaperones, and a teacher toured the residential school. We saw dormitories where the children slept and the kitchen and dining hall where children worked and ate. I remember looking through a chain link fence at a group of boys playing softball. It was a suffocating, hot, dry day in late June. As the boys ran around the bases, clouds of dust hung in the air.

We were not allowed to talk to the kids. They were on display for us to look at only. In *They Called Me Number One*, Bev Sellars' book about her life in residential school, she recounts endless cruelties residential school children endured — such as being strapped for bedwetting — and how demeaning it felt when the white kids on field trips were brought through the facilities to view the captured Indigenous children. As an eleven-year-old child I knew this was all wrong. There we were dressed in summer clothes with our parents, who could afford to fund a field trip that was an hour and a half drive away, looking at the Indigenous children dressed in dark, drab uniforms. We were shown caged human beings who had been taken away from their families. Every day the children were told what they were was wrong, that they had to change and had to become something else. Does this sound familiar? The Duck Lake Indian Residential School closed in 1996, the last residential school to close in Canada. The long-term psychological and sociological damage created in residential schools will take generations to repair. The LGBT community has been damaged in many of the same ways.

I BECAME INVOLVED IN LGBT issues because I have a gay son who first faced open institutionalized discrimination in high school when he tried to donate blood. The same-sex marriage debate catapulted me into activism when the Canadian government began debating same-sex marriage legislation in the early 2000s. By 2005 some Albertans launched a mean-spirited campaign to block same-sex marriage in our province. The LGBT community needed the support of outspoken supportive straight allies, and legislators had to hear from all citizens, not just isolated minority or special interest groups. I wanted both of my children to have identical rights and recognized it was necessary for me to take a public stand. Anything else was unthinkable. I could not sit back and watch, pretending it wasn't happening. LGBT issues are a part of basic human rights that affect all of us. I had a secure job and an understanding employer, and my husband and sons were supportive and recognized the need for public advocacy. I was driven to take a stand, to publicly acknowledge I had a gay son, celebrate every part of him and defend his right to have equal status in our country. I wasn't going to stand by and watch while anyone hurled anything at Carl or our family or tried to block Carl's right to equal treatment in this country.

Initially I was hurt and saddened by the anti-same-sex-marriage articles and letters to the editor I read in the newspaper. Over a few weeks, my sadness turned into disbelief, then anger, which forced me to actively campaign in support of equal treatment on marriage issues. I wrote letters, made phone calls, and attended town halls and protest rallies, marched in the Pride Parade and arranged dinners and meetings with politicians and civic leaders. The following year Kris Wells, Andre Grace, and I met with the provost at the University of Alberta to initiate planning for a campus-wide safe-space program for students and staff. Next I organized PFLAG panels during Pride Week with the hope of getting LGBT individuals and their families out to an event where they would find a supportive community. In 2008 when I started my position as general manager of the University of Alberta Devonian Botanic Garden, we actively promoted inclusion by adding a little inverted rainbow triangle to our website pages and print materials and began hosting official Pride Week activities and events. Every year I saw more and more same-sex couples walking hand-in-hand around the garden as the location became known within the LGBT community as a welcoming and safe space.

These were small but important gestures of inclusion. For too long the LGBT community was made to feel like they didn't belong, that they had to hide or pretend they were something else. North American society must accept that in some cases older LGBT individuals will never fully trust the general public's actions and will always keep their guard up in case they need to retreat to protect themselves. This is what happens when discrimination is all you have known throughout your life. Federal and provincial legislation and human rights policies have been rewritten to protect and promote equality, and our public schools have inclusion policies. It's society's turn to openly demonstrate inclusion, which can be done by displaying something as simple as a little rainbow flag in shops and restaurant windows, on church signs, and on websites.

THIS WAS JUST THE start for me. I will always have a gay son and LGBT issues have become part of my day-to-day life. I am hopeful someday soon the LGBT community will no longer have to come out.

For centuries gay people were forced to be invisible, hiding who they were. Society has begun moving to the other extreme where in 2016 LGBT adolescents, teenagers, and adults feel pressured to publicly disclose deeply personal facts about themselves. Students are forced to deal with their classmates' reactions in person and online. Professional American football player Michael Sam's coming out was broadcast to millions as the international media scrutinized him.

Carl's initial coming out coincided with the onset of massive shifts in the definition of a traditional family. The day Carl came out to me, his sadness about not being able to have a family had reached hopeless despair. Through adoption, surrogacy, and same-sex marriage legislation a variety of family structures have become more visible and have evolved to include families of same-sex couples. Homosexuality will be commonplace when kids, with heterosexual parents, grow up going to school and playing with kids, who live on their street or in their building, that have two dads or two moms. Kids don't need explanations, nor do they try to change their friends. They just want to play. They accept their friends as they are. This generation of children will grow up knowing families include homes with same-sex parents. The arrangement will not be unique or unfamiliar to them. When these kids become parents their children will have to be told there was a time when same-sex marriage and LGBT families were unheard of or kept secret. In Canada it will take a couple of generations for LGBT individuals and their families to be freed from a history of discrimination and oppression. I am hopeful a complete societal shift will happen in my lifetime.

Leonard and I didn't suspect we had an LGBT child. Upon learning I had a gay son, I thought, and feared, this would mean everything was going to change. In reality only one aspect of Carl's personal life is different than what I assumed was the case until the day he came to see me in my office when he was in grade eleven. How I feel about my son has not changed. Nothing changed regarding his dad's and my relationship with him. We love our sons, always have and always will. I want my children to be happy and both are happy. One is straight and one is gay.

I would have liked it if Carl would have married Meghan, or Caroline, the girl he said he wanted to marry when they were five years old. Of course, none of this could have come to pass, and really, how often does it happen that you select a life partner based on your parents' recommendations? My parents wanted me to marry a Ukrainian Catholic boy.

My life took a completely unexpected turn after learning I had a gay son. I was inspired by his courage. It took guts for him to come out in high school and it took resolve and stamina for him to create the GSA.

My deep love for my son challenged me to confront my own fear and paranoia about homosexuality and how it is perceived in North America. The open homophobic language that was used by every age group throughout my life until recently is now confined mostly to senior citizens and junior high school students. Homophobic language doesn't fly the way it used to.

It's been over a decade of advocacy, brunches, parades, fundraising, PFLAG meetings, and phone calls and discussions about LGBT issues. I actively promote the workplace as a safe space for everyone. My engagement with the LGBT community has deepened my love with Leonard, Carl, and Paul.

Before December 2002, it had never occurred to me that I would go out of my way to get to know and actively support the LGBT community. I now keep track of public figures and elected officials who do and don't attend Pride events. I've ended relationships based on individuals' use of what they refer to as colourful language and what I regard as homophobic language.

Initially I felt alone, so I called the gay and lesbian centre, I checked the "Queer" section in newspapers and magazines, Leonard and I attended PFLAG meetings. All of these things helped me realize we were not alone. Every gay person has parents and odds are their parents are asking the same questions and have the same concerns as my husband and me. We quickly found out other parents, families, and friends felt like we did. In order to cope, we deny the thoughtlessness we see in fellow human beings will ever be used to harm our children. At the same time we worry that our children will be irreparably damaged by cruelty and cry when we're reminded we can't live their lives for them or protect them forever.

Although I might not know who you are and I likely don't know why you are reading this book, understand this: you are not alone. My wish is that everyone who struggles with similar fears can address those fears and meet them head on. I've learned through experience that it will give you strength. You have my support and we don't even know each other. There are millions of families with LGBT kids, all of whom need their parents' love and acceptance. Hold your children and tell them you love them.

III

Scona Pride

It's wednesday, november 25, 2015. winter arrived two days ago with a huge dump of snow and below freezing temperatures. Fall was so warm this year my sweet peas were blooming on November 1 and I still had snapdragons blooming this week. This isn't normal in this part of the country. I'm not sure whether I should celebrate or worry that it's further evidence of global warming.

At noon today the temperature is minus eight degrees Celsius. I'm at Strathcona High School to speak to Scona Pride, formerly known as the Diversity Club, the gay-straight alliance Carl started nearly twelve years ago. Ms. Matthews, one of the original five teachers in the room at the first meeting in February 2004, has invited me to speak to the students about how the club started, what it was like when Carl came out, and how our family reacted.

I arrive half an hour early to look around the school hoping to say hi to a few teachers who might still be on staff. After driving back and forth through the west parking lot I find an open spot along the fence by the track. I feel a bit anxious walking up to the school this morning, not only because I'll be flat on my back if I take a wrong step in a parking lot that is slippery with packed snow but because this is where it all started when Carl was determined to come out and create a high school GSA.

In 2002, nearly thirteen years ago, Carl would have driven to school, parked in the same parking lot I'm in, and gone in through the west gym doors. On December 4 of that year he called me from school to say he needed to see me in my office. He came out to me that specific day because the burden of having a secret had become too much for him to bear. Carl was sixteen years old, he felt alone, he hadn't found the youth group at the Pride Centre yet and he didn't know there were supportive teachers at his school. He heard "so gay" a hundred times a day at school and, sadly, there were times he heard it from one of his teachers.

I know I'll meet students today who haven't been able to come out to their parents; some may be questioning their sexuality, others will be dealing with transgender issues. As I cautiously manoeuvre through the parking lot I wonder how many kids I'll see this morning that feel the same angst Carl felt when he was their age.

I go in through the same west gym doors, just like I had done for six years while my sons were students here, and immediately notice the school's made upgrades since my last visit. The exterior glass doors are new and the fifties-era lime green ceramic tile hallway walls and all of the lockers have been painted a gorgeous rich, dark grey. A phys. ed. teacher, who I don't recognize, is speaking quietly to a class of boys sitting on the stairs leading to the main gym. I round the corner and see my sons' Social Studies teacher, who greets me and asks me to say hello to my sons. Okay, this is beginning to feel really good, I think to myself. It's at least eight years since I last saw the man and he recognizes me and remembers my name. Nice. I stop to look through the trophy cases searching for Paul's name on the Scarborough Leadership Trophy. As luck would have it, the side with the 2007 plaque isn't facing the front of the showcase this year. The school feels familiar and I know my way around but when I turn around to go to the office I forget to be careful not to step on the school crest inlaid into the floor by the main front doors, violating a long-standing tradition. Student services is in a new location across the hall from the renovated office. Both areas are bright and open with floor to ceiling interior glass walls so anyone inside or walking by can see straight through.

At the office, I'm immediately greeted as I walk up to the counter.

"Mrs. Swanson. I would have recognized you anywhere. How are the boys?" Now I'm beginning to feel like a celebrity. (I found out later the office staff had been told to expect me.)

I spend a few minutes visiting with an assistant principal and the teacher who was the students' union coordinator when Paul was SU president and Carl was vice president. Both of them are eager to get an update on my sons. One of them tells me she has a little girl who is four years old. The bell rings and it's lunchtime. I wait outside the office for Ms. Matthews. We wind our way through the kids as they get lunches from their lockers and take the stairs to the second floor. There are fifteen hundred students in this school but it doesn't feel as packed as I remember and seems calm in the hallways. In the classroom where the GSA is meeting, dry marker white boards have replaced the chalk blackboards.

A little over a decade ago my son could have been one of the kids coming into the room. I look around, studying the faces, and realize Carl started the Diversity Club when the oldest student here was five years old. Some of them weren't even in kindergarten in 2002. In spite of the time that's gone by I feel like each student could be my own son or daughter. Some students might have a parent who feels exactly the same way I felt when Carl first came out. I've spoken in over fifty university classes. The Scona Pride students are not only four or five years younger than the university students, this room is populated by students that are either LGBT themselves or have someone very important in their life that is gay. Everything I'm about to speak to applies directly to their everyday experience.

Ms. Matthews introduces me to the twenty-five students and four teachers who sit eating their lunches. I tell them a little bit about PFLAG and how Carl took a year to come out to his dad, me, and then Paul, and how secrets can destroy your soul. I reenact my telephone conversation with my mother and her reaction, and stress how important it was for me to have my mom's support. I tell them how Carl and I battled about his wanting to come out in high school and that I was opposed to him even thinking about starting a GSA. After I read the GSA proposal Carl wrote to the principal I ask if there are any questions. A student says, "How can I help my friend who can't come out to his parents?"

"You can't make anyone come out," I say. "Your friend will know when the time is right and he is ready. Everyone has to come out on his or her own terms; he'll know when he's at that point. Having a good support system is very important. All you can do is be there for your friend and support him." I tell them about Paul's friend who came out to his friends before he could come out to his parents and think to myself, I knew it, ten years have gone by and kids still struggle with coming out to their parents. I look around the room, hoping for more questions. Twenty-five teenage angels sit transfixed, watching me. A few awkward seconds go by, then Ms. Matthews invites me to tell the class about Carl's night terrors in grade ten. I recall the night Carl kicked a hole in the wall in his sleep; the episode where he rolled down an entire flight of stairs without waking up; how he stood in the middle of my mother's living room screaming nonsense at two thirty in the morning; and how the night terrors stopped as unexpectedly as they started. "Carl came out to his dad three months later." The room grows even quieter and no one flinches.

I'm used to university students who always have at least a few questions. These kids seem shy, almost self-conscious. I'm not sure what to do next so I ask how it feels to have a GSA at school. To my relief, five hands shoot up simultaneously.

The first student says, "It's great to have a place where you don't have to explain anything. I describe myself as a-romantic. Everyone in this room knows what that means." Everyone nods in agreement and I don't let on that I don't know what a-romantic means.

"My parents are really supportive, but I was questioning in grade ten," says another student. "It's nice to come here and not have to be in the hallways every lunch hour."

The others make similar comments. It's part of their school life. They speak with such self-assurance that I don't know if it's ever occurred to them that this wasn't always the case or that there are high schools in Alberta without GSAS. The fact that something didn't exist twelve years ago is ancient history for a sixteen-year-old but the same timespan for me feels like only yesterday. I'm beginning to see the students haven't given much thought to Carl's trailblazing, and why should they? For them it's normal to have a GSA. Suddenly I think back to the 2004 Pride

Awards ceremony where Carl and two students from another Edmonton high school were awarded Pride Certificates as founders of GSAs. The presenters were giddy as they described the award and the recipients, saying that when they were high school students they didn't think this could happen in their lifetime. The presenters rejoiced and celebrated Carl and the other students. The 2015 Scona students take the existence of the club for granted — as they should.

The lunch break is almost over. I have time to ask one more question. "How many times a day do you hear 'so gay?'" The room erupts. Everyone in the entire group starts talking to me at the same time. I can't understand a word. It takes a few seconds for the frenzy to die down.

While some do say they hear "so gay" frequently, it seems that overall most students hardly ever hear the phrase at Scona. I'm relieved to hear a shift happens between the grade seven experience Avram told me about and the high school experience at Scona. The willingness of grade seven students to try out slang and casual insults appears to be adolescent behaviour, not something for the more mature high school, with the exception of a minority who might not be that socially aware.

The bell rings, lunch hour is over. The students applaud and leave the room. They file past me, smile, and say thank you.

My feeling of celebrity lasted for about 15 minutes. I thought there would be interest in the obstacles Carl had to get past to actually get the GSA started and had prepared for that discussion. The GSA's history appeared to be irrelevant. How the GSA got started didn't matter to the 2015 students. To them it had always been there. Over the years the name had changed several times to better reflect the particular perspective and interests of the students involved.

It occurred to me that the school had changed on multiple levels. The equipment and facilities had been updated and improved, but also, the kids in Scona Pride had been born into a better time and in a more supportive society. The students have no memory of the same-sex marriage debate; after all, it happened when most of them were preschoolers.

So, what's next? It's still extremely difficult to be transgender and people still can't get their head around bisexuals. But things are evolving. You can't lose your job or your apartment anymore because you are gay. Our children have LGBT role models. In Canada we have openly gay police officers and politicians. The premier of Ontario is a married lesbian and Winnipeg had a gay mayor a few years ago. In 2015 Ireland legalized same-sex marriage by popular vote. Professional athletes and high profile corporate executives such as Tim Cook at Apple are starting to come out and no one even talks about Ellen DeGeneres or Neil Patrick Harris's sexuality anymore. HIV/AIDS is no longer a death sentence in western countries. The plotlines in mainstream LGBT TV sitcoms have shifted from focusing on the sophisticated gay professional in *Will and Grace* to the trials and tribulations of parenthood in *Modern Family*. Hollywood movies *Brokeback Mountain* and *Milk* received many award nominations and both won several Academy Awards. Pride parades and the after-parties are now civic celebrations with corporate sponsors and bouncy castles in the family play area. In 2015 the Canadian military led Edmonton's Pride Parade.

It still isn't easy and there will always be homophobes just as there will always be racists, but thankfully, today's LGBT community lives in a better Canada and LGBT youth have benefitted from their predecessors' hard-fought battles and subsequent victories. It's up to all of us to make sure we do everything we can to keep moving forward to ensure what's been accomplished is never lost.

About the Author

Ruby Remenda Swanson was born and raised in Humboldt, Saskatchewan and is a graduate of the University of Saskatchewan. Ruby's early career began in educational radio and television at ACCESS Alberta. She freelanced as a publicist with the Children's Television Workshop in New York City and was the Community Relations Coordinator at the Canadian Broadcasting Corporation in Edmonton. For six years Ruby was at home with her two beautiful little boys as a full-time parent and homemaker. When the boys grew older she worked evenings as the Teacher/Coordinator of an English as a Second Language program for new immigrants to Canada. Following a stint in politics as the Constituency Office Manager for the Leader of the Official Opposition of Alberta during the late 90s, Ruby joined the University of Alberta. Since 2008 Ruby has been the General Manager of the University of Alberta Devonian Botanic Garden.

In 2004 and twice in 2014 Ruby volunteered and was selected to be part of the Government of Canada's Election Observer Mission in Ukraine. In 2016 she visited Ukraine with her son Paul, who is a professional commercial photographer. Together with their driver, Yarema Sirko, they travelled to rural areas in western Ukraine to visit the four ancestral villages her great grandparents left when they immigrated to Canada nearly 120 years ago. While in Kyiv, Lviv, and Ternopil, Ruby met with LGBT parent and youth groups, human rights workers and Canadian Embassy staff.